T5-AXE-033

security from above

CHARLES H. SCHMITZ

security from above

BIBLICAL THOUGHTS ON ULTIMATE VALUES

new york nashville ABINGDON PRESS

SECURITY FROM ABOVE

Library of Congress Catalog Card Number: 66-10851

SET UP, PRINTED, AND BOUND BY THE PARTHENON PRESS, AT NASHVILLE, TENNESSEE, UNITED STATES OF AMERICA

DEDICATED TO

my grandchildren . . .

Jodi

Scott

Steven

Contents

Work

Love

Body

Security

Security

> *For whoever would save his life will lose it; and whoever loses his life for my sake and the gospel's will save it*—Mark 8:35.

Security and insecurity are a pair of opposites that depend on each other. Security is based in insecurity! A child is secure because he is a child.

Everything about life in this world indicates insecurity. Nothing is fixed, so nothing is secure. You may be a very beautiful woman now, or a very handsome man now—but not for very long. Beauty fades, age takes over. Every organ of the body is made of fragile stuff. The body itself returns to dust, no matter what you do to prevent it.

No relationships in this life are fixed: husband to wife, wife to husband, parents to children, children to parents—all relationships are tentative, dependent, insecure. Every office you hold, every position you accept, has time limits and so is quite insecure in its very nature.

All the material possessions you accumulate exist in a climate of uncertainty. To increase your possessions is but to make an effort away from security, not toward it. Said Jesus, "Do not lay up for yourselves treasures on earth, where moth and rust consume and where thieves break in and steal, but lay up for yourselves treasures in heaven, where neither moth nor rust consumes and where thieves do not break in and steal. For where your treasure is, there will your heart be also" (Matt. 6:19-21).

Only when you are thoroughly insecure do you discover the false assumptions upon which life in this world rests, and only then are you ready to pick up and use your faith. You have faith at its keenest and best when you are most insecure. This faith is your security amid your insecurity.

Think of Jesus. Jesus' home life was quite insecure. He said of himself, "Foxes have holes, and birds of the air have nests; but the Son of man has nowhere to lay his head" (Matt. 8:20). Jesus' financial life was insecure. He had no steady income, no guaranteed wage, no unemployment insurance, no stocks, no bonds. Jesus' friends became sources of insecurity. Judas betrayed him, Peter denied him three times, Thomas had doubts about him, and all the rest forsook him and fled at a time when he needed them most. The government of his day, through a policy of appeasement, added to Jesus' insecurity by arresting him, trying him, scourging him, crucifying him. The title given Jesus—that of "King of the Jews" (Matt. 27:37)—was but a grim insecure mockery. On the cross—totally insecure, as men measure security—he was most secure, saying, "Father, into thy hands I commit my spirit" (Luke 23:46). He lost his life, in order to save it, in order to secure it.

When events of your life proceed from insecurity, then—if you are a Christian—you can feel secure! The person whose security depends on worldly attachments cannot know God as God may be known. Religious experience provides the only worthy security based in insecurity. If your security lies in your looks, your family, your home, your position, your bank account, your government, then life is nothing but insecurity, because life is change. The person who thinks he is secure in these worldly areas has little or no religious experience.

The conversion experience is the focus of security! To open your life to God and Christ is to let security in. To close your life to God is to invite insecurity. The effort must be put forth to open life to God so that when trouble comes (even a crucifixion) you can go back to the religious experience, and put yourself again in the presence of God. Security is the climax of your own personal effort to seek and find God present within yourself. Security at its best comes from within and not from without—not from things, but from the spirit. Security cannot possibly come from an atomic fallout shelter. Security comes from an honest recognition of the world as it is and eternal life as it can be.

Security comes not from a sense of time, but from a sense of timelessness. Your security does not lie in your age, whether you are eighteen or thirty-eight or fifty-eight or seventy-eight years old. Security lies in the path to God, not the path to self. The short-cut to security lies in a profound religious experience: a conversion, a born-again experience—readying you for inner peace and security. There must be an effort toward God, just as there has been an effort toward self. "Work out your own salvation with fear and trembling; for God is at work in you" (Phil. 2:12-13). Remember always and in all ways that "whoever would save his life will lose it; and whoever loses his life for my sake and the gospel's will save it. For what does it profit a man, to gain the whole world and forfeit his life?" (Mark 8:35-36).

Two Invisible Specks

> *It does not yet appear what we shall be*—I John 3:2.

Before you were conceived you were but two tiny specks, invisible to the naked eye. In due time you came out of your mother's body into the world—a living child.

From two invisible specks to a child: a child with a brain, two eyes, two ears, a mouth, a nose, and everything else, to create this mysterious YOU with infinite possibilities. At birth your body and soul had all the equipment to someday become a full-grown person of a hundred pounds or more, and of a thousand skills or more. The two invisible specks were more, much more than they seemed to be.

You are an adult now, knowledgeable and wise. You sometimes assume that you have reached the limit of your capabilities. However, it is still true that you can be much more than you are. The difference between what you now are and what you yet may be could very well be as great as the difference between the two invisible specks you once were and what you now are. There are no limits as to what you may become here and hereafter.

An ancient writer put it this way "It does not yet appear what we shall be." He presented this intriguing thought not while he was thinking of himself at the beginning of life, but rather, while he was thinking of himself in maturity. Even in his later years, he was persuaded that appearances had not yet disclosed the greatness within him.

"Beloved, we are God's children now; it does not yet appear what we shall be, but we know that when he appears we shall be like him, for we shall see him as he is." As a child of the eternal God at this very moment, think and then think again about the more that you already have become from two invisible specks, the more that you are becoming, and the more you will yet become—all from just two invisible specks.

"It does not yet appear what we shall be"—not yet. Not yet!

Time

> *You know how to interpret the appearance of earth and sky; but why do you not know how to interpret the present time?*—Luke 12:56.

The time within you is unlike the time for anyone else. It is a different time within every human being. You know not what time it is for yourself. How can you then tell time for another?

You say you tell time by the clock, but the face of the clock may deceive you. You say you tell time by the calendar, but that too is man's invention and is in error. You may tell time by your body, and yet the weakest moment of your flesh may be your strongest hour.

Time passes; it never arrives. Time goes; it never

comes. Time is a nervous patient on edge, shaking and being shaken, always impending. Time is a cloud that moves across your sky, taking different shapes and forms, obscuring the sun while it helps you to look into its face.

Where is time? It is here and there and everywhere. It is a flowing part of you and you are a moving part of it. You cannot take hold of it, and yet, you may redeem it. You cannot lift it, and yet, it may lift you. While it is day for you, it is night for another. That place in the world in which you find yourself determines in part what time it is for you.

You have time, and yet, you know not how much. You have life, yet, you know not how long. Master time before it masters you. Make each day as a thousand years of living. Create and make decisions that will produce a good harvest. Do not make a god of time, but make it your servant. Time is yours, yet you know not what is truly yours until you redeem it.

You may not choose what to do with next year. It is uncertain. You can choose what to do with *now*. You may turn the present into fat or energy, waste or values. Channel time to life and more life. Make time immortal by redeeming it for immortality. You cannot redeem another's time; you can redeem only your own.

Time is so utterly individual. Think well and think clearly about time. We were not born together, nor will we die together. The years given each person are different years. Ultimately there is no common clock and no common calendar. Discover what time it is for *you,* what it may do for *you,* and what *you* may do for it. Your time is unlike time for anyone else. Discover the "more" in time for you—the security of timelessness in the midst of time.

Change

> *And we all, with unveiled face, beholding the glory of the Lord, are being changed into his likeness from one degree of glory to another*—II Cor. 3:18.

You can never be the same again! Your body will never return to what it was when you were a child. Your mind can never be what it was yesterday because you have lived another day.

The ideals of your childhood are not the ideals you possess now. The ideals you will possess a year from now will be modified by the fifty-two weeks that will come and go. Your life is fluid; it is forever in motion. You are a part of something that is always ongoing. Do not resist the very essence of life itself.

The world is never normal, nor are you. You wake up each morning a somewhat different person in a somewhat different world. You are not a metal mold within a metal mold. You are a creative human being in a creative world.

Why try so hard to be the same again under conditions where that is utterly impossible? Are you guarding something that is no longer there? Are you cherishing a treasure that has lost its value in a different time and a different world? Do not try to remain as you were when life offers you a succession of changes.

You will always be a pilgrim and a stranger here. There is no continuing city, no continuing church, no sameness anywhere. Do not try to live only in the yesterdays as if there were no todays and no tomorrows.

You are a growing child in a growing world. You need to be born anew with each new day. You are a part of the continuing resurrection and life within and without you. You would be most unhappy were life to be one continuing round of yesterdays. There would be no need for faith and hope in a world where you could be the same again.

Because you do live in a changing world, you live in a world that is not damned. A changing world is a saving world. A world that lives is a redeemable world. To a world that is new each morning, there comes fresh mercies suitable to the changed day.

A shifting world is not a den of thieves; it is only a shifting world. Strive not for the past, or you may strive for death and not for life.

Change is your friend and not your enemy. Do not deny your friend, but give him your best. Look to the past with forgetting. Embrace each day with tomorrow's dream that you may come to know yourself—your larger self, your newer more mature self.

Dreams

> *We shall see what will become of his dreams*—Gen. 37:20.
>
> *And Joseph remembered the dreams which he had dreamed*—Gen. 42:9.

Wake not from your dreams lest the waking find you dying. Your dreams would disclose you to yourself. Hide not your dreams from your uttermost being, your full maturity.

The world knows you not because it knows not your dreams. The most intimate life of your being is veiled from others. Unveil it not, lest others laugh you to scorn while they silently nourish their own dreams.

Your inner life is more real than the life the world sees and knows. The joy you feel is not the less real because you only dream of it. Were that joy to become flesh, it might cease to be joy. Your inner light is the real light of your life. Within you there is a foretaste of heaven. The taste is good; deny it not. Let your dreams bless you and keep you.

Watch over your dreams, lest age take them from you. Remain a child in your innermost being. Give yourself to the bosom of your dreams—make not a fool of them. Enjoy the child within you more than once!

Your dreams will never deceive you. They will never betray you nor deny you. The real world knows deceit, betrayal, denial—the inner world of your dreams knows them not. Try your dreams—they will never leave you nor forsake you.

Dreams are the creation of faith, hope, and love. Out of this trinity of being dreams come to be. There is an hour for the dreams whose time has come to go into the real world. The ages may have had the dream and kept it, until all was ready for it. Faith, hope, and love conceive through the ages and wait for the fullness of time to give birth to the dream. The innermost then becomes the uttermost. The struggles for the dream are vindicated. The dream comes out of the womb of mortality into immortality. Men look upon the dream and marvel, forgetting it once was "only a dream."

All creation—the kingdom of God—was once "only a dream."

Wake not from your dreams, lest the waking find you dying. Within you, creation works upon another dream—the dream of the *more* within you, the ultimate security.

Faith

> *Now faith is the assurance of things hoped for, the conviction of things not seen*—Heb. 11:1.

Faith is a gift you buy for yourself (not another) in the markets of personal experience (Heb. 11). You may never know the nature of this gift, nor may you ever know what you really paid for it. However, you will someday know what it has created for you, when life itself tells you so.

Faith has no eyes, and yet it has vision—it sees more than eyes can see. Faith is numb and yet it can feel more than the senses may allow. When you speak most of faith, then you may be in doubt of it. Faith has nothing to boast of, for it possesses nothing and yet has everything.

Your faith is peculiarly, uniquely your own—you bought it for yourself. Your faith fits only you, your nature, your individuality, your deepest self—so do not try to make your most intimate personal faith fit another. Your faith clothes your body, your mind, your past, your future. There is no "common faith," no assembly-line edition of faith; there can be only the faith of each person: an unrepeated faith.

Faith is a growing gift slowly coming to maturity when you are honest with yourself, with your deep convictions. Then faith fills the gaps of your childish self. A maturing faith with patience and truth slowly fills the empty rooms in the mansion of the soul.

To ask what faith is, is to ask a question. Faith may not freely ask questions because this is not quite in keeping with the essential nature of faith. Faith may make no requests for information. Faith may seek no answers because answers may wait on faith. Answers come to faith. Answers may not necessarily come to just questions.

The faith you possess has a greatness about it that makes it larger than your body, more expansive than your soul. The only boundary faith has is an unknown boundary—heaven itself.

Faith is a growing gift you have bought for yourself (not another) in the markets of experience. It is a gift out of which other gifts are born. The child of faith is hope. The child of faith is love. Faith ever gives. It must give in order to live.

Faith can be kept but it cannot be stored. Faith never surrenders; it is not the nature of faith to ever give up. Faith never gives battle, and yet it ultimately wins the victory. Faith can only stand; it has no way of sitting down.

Guard well your growing, maturing faith. Let no one take it from you. Let no new experience shrivel it. Let no form of words make its meaning void for you. Walk with your faith toward life and more life. Let your faith unfold you to yourself. Let it give you of itself while it uncovers the kingdom of God for you.

Creativity

> *I was a stranger and you welcomed me*—Matt. 25:35.

Try as you will, you find it hard to be creative. You seem only to modify the old and to choose the familiar path. But you do want to be creative. You want to originate ideas and things. You want to be a creator together with God. But how? How? Creativity escapes you.

You say you are not intelligent enough to be creative, but intelligence as such is not the basic ingredient of creativity. All intellectuals are not creative. All creative individuals are not highly intellectual.

If you want to be creative, keep your heart and mind open to new experiences. Do not be afraid to engage life in strange places and in unusual times. The more you limit yourself to what you have always known the less you are likely to be creative. See as much as you can. Live as much as possible. Learn while you live. Be bold and seek adventure. Creativity does not take place in a vacuum.

Do not label each new experience and file it away—this is foolish. Each new experience is a bridge—don't build a house on it. Every new adventure can be an opportunity for creativity. Bring each fresh experience to bear upon your life. Recombine it with other experiences and so relate it to the world that it will form a new pattern for you. Every new experience is a raw experience brought into your life to be sharpened and reinterpreted into a new idea or a new thing. Creativity is limited only by what you do with new experiences.

Where you live has much to do with whether you are creative or not. Your daily environment will either dull you or make you freshly aware. The house you live in can suffocate the new, or invite the new to be born in you. Your friends can stimulate or anesthetize you. If you persist in living where life goes along at a dying rate, you will never become creative. Choose the best place to live. Find the right friends with whom to associate. In this way will you be more likely to become creative.

Develop a habit of discovery, of discovering the stranger. Become interested in new meanings, new implications, fresh aesthetic values, new persons. Keep your emotions clean and sensitive toward yourself, toward your environment, and toward others. Do not expect to find very much that is new in a crowd—crowds inhibit creativity. Crowds give themselves to staleness, not freshness. Crowds discover nothing; only individuals discover. Creativity is a race run one by one, never by a crowd, or even two by two.

Occasionally go into hiding with yourself and there in solitude make as many new connections between fresh experiences as you can. To be creative you must be willing to walk alone and think alone on occasion. So will you become more than you are. So will you become creative and secure.

Wakefulness

Awake, O sleeper . . .—Eph. 5:14.

When was the last time you were not quite awake? Most people are wide awake in the fullest sense only about one minute of every hour! You are usually only half awake. You are usually somewhere between sleep and wakefulness.

You have blackouts of attention. Your mind wanders. How often do you stand before a door marked "Push" and pull instead? How much of what you read do you really absorb? Did you know that the human eye can spot about two thousand stars from first (brightest) to sixth magnitudes on a clear night? Now, how many stars have you seen in your whole life, and yet you can see about two thousand stars on one clear night.

You are awake if you *welcome new and worthy ideas.* Because something has been done a certain way for decades or even centuries does not necessarily make it right or good. You are awake if you continue through new times to redefine your reason for living, never assuming that the reason you had for living when you were a child is altogether valid as the reason for living when you have become a grown person. You are awake if throughout your life you remain a learner, never assuming you have arrived at all knowledge. Remember always that "our knowledge is imperfect and and our prophecy is imperfect"—(I Cor. 13:9). Remember always and in all ways that "Now I know in part"—(I Cor. 13:12).

You are awake if you will *"Make love your aim,* and earnestly desire the spiritual gifts"—(I Cor. 14:1). Love will keep you fully awake.

There is something else you need to know about

wakefulness, and that is *go into a contest with yourself*. Do not go into a contest with someone else, only with yourself. In Japan, archery is a contest of the archer with himself. Archery is used to train the mind to be at one with the goal, a truly spiritual goal. Fundamentally the marksman aims at himself —the aimer and the aim at one simultaneously. Bow and arrow are only a pretext for something happening within.

You are in this life in a contest with yourself—to be better than you now are, than you now think you can be. The archer trains his mind to be fully awake, aimer and aim at one, completely aware. So will you too become fully awake when you as a Christian aim toward the *mature* Christ within you (not the baby Jesus). So in wakefulness will you become more than you now are.

Jesus

Jesus

Consider Jesus—Heb. 3:1.

Jesus can tell you much about the *more* within you. Consider him!

Jesus did not demand the same of every person. As far as we know he said, "You must be born anew" (John 3:7) only to Nicodemus.

Jesus loved children, but he was no baby-sitter spending his time wiping noses and overseeing afternoon naps. He never tried to find a child before it was lost. He never answered questions that were not being asked.

Jesus had faith in individuals through their differences, knowing that no two persons could ever be alike. Jesus never asked "How can you be more like me?" He said "Follow me" but expected that each disciple would remain distinctively himself, while following him.

He knew that people listened to him for different reasons at different levels of understanding. He was always informal—as informal as a child. Jesus knew the will of God but he never played providence to himself.

Jesus knew that some of the worst sins flourished in that wide area between the ten commandments. No commandment pointed out the sins of jealousy, pride, indifference—the major sins of religious leaders. So Jesus framed two all-embracing commandments saying, "You shall love the Lord your God with all your heart, and with all your soul, and with all your mind. . . . You shall love your neighbor as yourself" (Matt. 22:37-39).

Jesus never confused the best with the Tower of Babel, the tower of words. He knew that religion could easily be reduced to exclusive expression in verbal forms. He knew that word managing skills could be mistaken for religion by the uninformed. So the Tower of Babel fell when "the Word became flesh and dwelt among us, full of grace and truth" (John 1:14).

Jesus was intelligent but he was not an intellectual. He was a teacher but not an educator as we now know educators. Jesus won individuals through the utter simplicity of his life and teaching. He never taught a new word! He shared the way, the truth, and the life so each could understand as a child and as a man. The little he wrote received a rejection slip from the sands of time.

Jesus sought to unveil and disclose the more and the sources of security within each person. He would uncover the more within you while you refuse to save your own life and give yourself in full service to others. Reconsider him and you will learn much about yourself and about security from above.

Just Because

For God so loved the world—John 3:16.

Have you ever found it difficult to find a reason for your behavior? You like certain foods, but you do not know exactly why. You like them "just because" you like them. There are certain persons you love, even though they may be quite unlovable to others, but you love them without detailed specific reason— you love them "just because."

You make choices every day, and you make them

without defining the reasons. Your intuitions may play a part, your background and education may share, your religion may affect these important daily decisions—but in the final analysis you reach a decision for no clear-cut reason. You decide "just because."

"Just because" is not a bad reason at all, even if you cannot tag or label it. Reason has a reason that reason may not know. God does his mighty works without depending upon extensive research to build up a reasonable case! The "why" of any deed need not be defined to justify the deed. The deed itself may have a self-contained reason beyond the realm of reason.

The very first word in John 3:16 is an important word. "*For* God so loved the world that he gave his only Son, that whoever believes in him should not perish but have eternal life." Why did God do it? Why did God behave that way? The first word has the answer: "For." And what does "For" mean? It means "just because."

God must have searched for a reason why he loved you so much. Looks? No. Character? No. Finally God gave up trying to find the "why" of it. His only conclusion was that he had no real clearly defined reason. He looked at you and loved you very, very much "just because."

The only answer you can give to love without reason is to love right back. An ancient writer felt that this was the very best response, and so he said "We love, because he first loved us" (I John 4:19).

Always remember the first word of John 3:16—"For." Why should you remember it? "Just because!"

Chew

Take, eat; this is my body—Matt. 26:26.

Do you chew your food or do you just swallow it? A certain girl munched a bread crumb 679 times! Many of us eat under tension, eat when depressed, eat while we worry, eat in a hurry. The food we swallow without chewing becomes a dead weight within us. Even a crumb of bread can be chewed 679 times! So the bread serves its full purpose before and after swallowing.

A great meaningful thought, like food, may be swallowed without chewing. But then the thought is lost to the life we live. There are persons who receive great ideas without ever mulling over them, examining them, fitting them into the structure of their lives. There are other individuals whose total lives are changed by just an idea, perhaps an idea like "I can do all things in him who strengthens me" (Phil. 4:13).

A great life, like food, may become an event of history buried in antiquity, or it may become a source of making new history in the contemporary scene. So Jesus may be "swallowed" as a noble figure of the remote past, or the sayings of his life may be "chewed" until they nourish the present.

"Take, eat; this is my body" does not mean "Here is a tasteless pill to swallow." To fold Jesus up into capsule form and present him to yourself as the great prescription of history is but to find him as a meaningless hero of the past unsuitable for this electronics age. The Jesus of history may be utterly irrelevant to twentieth-century digestive systems.

"Take, eat; this is my body" does mean that the Christ of God has truth and life to share that may become "the bread of life" for any age, any person, any time. Try "chewing" the Beatitudes for awhile—get the Life out of them—let them be absorbed into your system. Take Jesus' commandment to love God with all your heart and soul and mind; take his commandment to love your neighbor as yourself, chew on it for awhile in all honesty—then digest these commandments until all your experiences reflect them. You can "chew" the sayings of Jesus more than 679 times until you get all the spiritual nourishment and strength that you need to live forever. "Take, eat," don't just swallow!

Jesus Is Dead

> *For as often as you eat this bread and drink the cup, you proclaim the Lord's death until he comes*
> —I Cor. 11:26.

You have heard it said repeatedly that Jesus is alive, but I say to you that Jesus is dead! A new proclamation is in order that "You proclaim the Lord's death until he comes." It is expressly because Jesus is dead that we declare it through Holy Communion.

Paul describes the purpose of sharing in the bread and the cup by saying "For as often as you eat this bread and drink the cup, you proclaim the Lord's death until he comes." Jesus wanted all his friends to continually realize then and now that he is dead—presently dead.

Does it disturb you? It should! You count all too heavily upon the idea that Jesus is alive and so will assume responsibility for ever so many things. You take for granted that he is Lord of all and will rescue every situation. But this is quite impossible because a dead man cannot be held accountable, and no truly living person will knowingly lean upon a dead man. It should disturb you very much that Jesus is dead—very much so.

You need to be disturbed by the truth repeatedly. "Do this, as *often* as you drink it. . . . For as *often* as you eat. . . ." It is so easy to forget that Jesus is dead. Memory needs to be awakened repeatedly. We readily forget to remember that life has gone out of the Master. He is dead.

Why remember Jesus' death? Because human nature is essentially the same now as it was then. While Jesus was living on earth with his friends, it had become a habit with them to turn all responsibility over to him. If the sick needed help, Jesus would take care of it. If the hungry needed to be fed, Jesus would find a way. If the truth needed to be told, Jesus would tell it. Whatever needed to be done, it was commonly assumed that Jesus would do it. Then when Jesus died on the cross and rose again to a new and different life, it was still the habit of his friends to "let Jesus do it." So the early church, like the present church, had to be constantly and consistently reminded of the simple, yet profound truth that Jesus is dead.

If Jesus is dead, who then is to do his work in the world? Paul tells us who in the twelfth chapter of I Corinthians, saying, "Now you are the body of Christ and individually members of it" (I Cor. 12:27). You are it now. Jesus is dead and you are to take his place in the world. You are the substitute *living* body of Jesus, taking the place of the dead body of Jesus here and now. No longer can any follower of Jesus say, "Let Jesus do it." You are the one and only body Jesus has now!

Remember Jesus is dead! In case you forget, partake of the Lord's Supper soon, and it will remind you again that Jesus is dead.

Presence

Lo, I am with you always—Matt. 28:20.

Your presence is requested! Through all the promising and the unpromising experiences that come to you, your presence is requested—*in full.* There may be times when you think you are present and really are not.

Just before the class was to assemble for a lecture the professor had to leave the room for a few moments. When the students arrived and found the professor was not in the classroom, they left, assuming that he had gone for the day. When the class assembled again the next day, the professor severely scolded the students, concluding his remarks by saying, "And remember, whenever you see my hat on this desk, you are to assume that I am present!" The class met again the following day and when the professor arrived, he noticed that there was a hat on each student's desk, but no students!

Your presence is requested. Are you honestly present when you give a contribution to a certain cause? Does that make you a part of the cause? Does money take the place of personal sharing? Do you consider yourself present in given situations through your wife or your husband or your children or your friends? Presence can mean very little or nothing when it is given in such token fashion.

What does it really mean to be present? It means you are there: in person, physically, mentally, spiritually. It means that you are fully participating and sharing in what is taking place. It means you are truly giving your full attention with everything that's under your hat—when you have your hat on! To be present in all of life's experiences is to glean from them every possibility of faith and hope and love. It is to make the occasion count toward growth and maturity.

Jesus said, "Lo, I am with you always." That means there is a Presence present in your presence. This Presence remains to be discovered and explored and claimed until every experience becomes a truly saving experience.

"Lo, I am with you always" means not only on particular occasions, such as Easter and Christmas and birthdays—but on all occasions, or in all ways, as well as always.

"Lo, I am with you always" denotes time and implies eternity. There is no stop to the presence of God, no pause or moment when he is not there. And he is there in full, completely.

Your presence is requested in an adequate sense to respond to the Presence with all that's under your hat when you have it on! In this Presence, present in your presence, lies the security from above.

Enemies

> *Thou preparest a table before me in the presence of my enemies*—Ps. 23:5.

With whom did you eat breakfast this morning? Was it with a friend or with an enemy? At first you suppose that only friends would eat together. Mealtime is no time to be with enemies, so you would conclude —but that conclusion may be wrong!

You need to *discover your enemies among your friends.* Enemies are not always where they are supposed to be. Some may be found behind the iron curtain, others behind the bamboo curtain, and others sitting beside you when you eat. Jesus discovered his enemies among his friends. When one of his most intimate friends rebuked Jesus, Jesus said to Peter, "Get behind me, Satan! You are a hindrance to me; for you are not on the side of God, but of men" (Matt. 16:23). Later, at the Last Supper, Jesus suggested that one of his friends would betray him. Each of his friends (no exceptions) began to say to him one after another, "Is it I, Lord?" Each friend honestly suspected himself as an enemy, until the betrayer was revealed among his friends. Discover your enemies among your friends.

You need to *discover your enemies among your relatives too.* Relatives may be well intentioned and yet be set against your ultimate good. Medical doctors nowadays send their patients to hospitals for a number of reasons, but sometimes a primary reason is to get them away from relatives who disobey the doctor's orders. In the hospital the patient may recover more rapidly than at home.

A cartoon showed an elderly lady sitting in a rocking chair with a smiling youngster on her lap. The caption under the cartoon gave the words of the youngster: "Grandma, you spoil me!" Find your enemies among your relatives.

A young lady had a very real religious experience in a church service. A short time afterward she got up in prayer meeting and testified: "Before I gave my heart to the Lord, I was foolish and vain. I loved beautiful clothes, expensive jewelry—but, my friends, when I saw that these things were dragging me down to hell, I gave them all to my sister!" Even through a noteworthy religious experience one may become the enemy of a relative. Discover your enemies among your friends and relatives and then learn another truth.

Discover that *you yourself are your own worst enemy.* Whenever you sit down to eat, even though it may be just a coffee break, you are sitting in the presence of your own worst enemy—yourself. "Thou preparest a table before me in the presence of my enemies" applies to the moment and to the near. The Apostle Paul understood this truth, saying, "I do not understand my own actions. For I do not do what I want, but I do the very thing I hate" (Rom. 7:15). Paul continues, "When I want to do right, evil lies close at hand" (Rom. 7:21). Paul knew that he had more trouble with himself than with anyone else—so do you.

What to do about it? Just to possess this insight is to come upon a new understanding of yourself. It is to reexamine the behavior of friends and relatives to find out where and when they became a drag and not a lift for you. It is to reexamine yourself and gain a worthy victory in the civil war going on inside you. It is to find the Master present as a Savior at every mealtime, as he was at the Last Supper, a Savior even among enemies.

Work

Work

> *We must work the works of him who sent me, while it is day: night comes, when no one can work*—John 9:4.

Make work the love of your life. Great literature, art, and music came to be through the labor of love and the love of labor. Make love the eyes within your labor that you may see its possibilities. Look well upon the universe, the masterpiece of creation. God made love the work of life—will you?

You who know only drudgery, fear, weakness—make work the love of your life and you will discover the high fidelity of being a partner with the Creator. The very high and the very low ranges of life's sweetest music come through labor—the love of labor and the labor of love. It is not good to work for work's sake, but work for the sake of love. Find your creative faithful best in making work the love of your life.

When you work, you are a harp through whose strings the past, present, and future may be heard. You may approach your work as one would a harp—from the left or right. Your work is not a one-sided venture. The strings of life are free, before and behind. You may do with them what you will. If you make work the love of life it will keep you in tune with the infinite.

When you work, you are a many-stringed instrument. Every thought, every experience, every "piece" of work is like a new string with new dimensions of being, added to your life. Each experience may be stretched taut (like a string) and then plucked at different levels to bring forth new music. Or, each experience may hang loose (like a string) in meaninglessness. Make work your love, creatively yielding much from the many-stringed instrument called your life.

Love and labor, labor and love are father and mother of life. Labor creates life when it is in love.

Stresses and strains are not in vain. Leave not work by itself, apart from you. Put love around your labor. Put love into your work, so will your labor become more than labor—you will become more than you are. You will not be one among many, but many in one—many more than you are.

Enter creation's story—become one with the Creator God. Make work the love of life and come to know the music of the heavens in true high fidelity.

You

> *The thief comes only to steal and kill and destroy; I came that they may have life, and have it abundantly*—John 10:10.

You are more, much more than you think you are. The full meaning of you is the goal of your life.

You are many things and many nothings. You are a child and a man. You are an individual and a crowd. You are the past, the present, and the future. You are a part of many worlds, yet you are a world all your own. Earth and heaven, night and day, meet in you.

Unfold yourself through the many things that you are. Discover the difference between the things and the nothings within and about you. Do not try to turn nothing into something, nor something into nothing. Set aside the nothings lest they shrink your life. Your fears are nothing; they are imaginary. Your age is nothing; you are eternal. Your gold is nothing; it cannot buy what you most need. Your enemies are nothing; they cannot reach your soul.

Your body is something; it is the seed in which you live and move and have your being. Your faith is something; it is the staff of life. Your love is something; it buys what you most need. Your friends are something; they help create you. Your thoughts are something; they unfold you to yourself.

You cannot truly see your full self in a mirror. In a mirror you see only your clothed self, clothed with flesh and garments. Your real reflection comes only through reflection. You reach your heart through your head; you reach your innermost by tapping your own reflective consciousness. Let yourself live. Do not lose yourself among the nothings. Find yourself among life's extras. Drink the wine of life until the cup is drained and the taste is hauntingly remembered.

You are more, you always will be—forever more. There is much in you that you have not made available to yourself. Look upon yourself, but not with tired eyes. Look upon yourself with freshness and wonder. Have faith in yourself through your faith in the Eternal. In *you* lie the ages curled up, ready to unfold at your bidding. *You* are the object of unfulfilled promises—waiting fulfillment. *You* are the prophet's dream. You are a little savior of the world.

You have been chosen for more; deny not your calling. The full meaning of *you* is the goal of your life.

First

> *But many that are first will be last, and the last first*—Mark 10:31.

There is no greater wisdom among those in first place than there is among those who are in the ranks. Those who are ahead seem to be wise because they become the subjects of flattery and praise. The mistakes of those who have priorities in this world are hidden by their associates. Half truths, silence, double-talk, diplomacy—these may cover the blunders of those who are in authority. Why do you then, wish to be in first place?

Is it because you want to have no one in front of you? Is it because you want to have your back to humanity? Is it because you forget that those who lead the parade of life are seldom honestly loved? Is it because you forget that to be first is to be in chains? Those who are first can seldom laugh!

Do you remember the churches that years ago dared to call themselves "First"? On the corner they stood back in the decades holding positions of true eminence. They were looked up to. Crowds flocked to them. Then times changed, and now the "first" is really the "last." All continued struggles to be first were in vain. But in becoming "last" instead of being "first" the noblest satisfaction may be found.

Strive not to be first, but strive to be last. You have not been called to be a statesman. You have been called to be a servant. Labor for the happiness and interest of others, not of yourself. If you must be first, be first in service, first to wash another's feet. If you must be first, be first in sincerity, first in purity of thought and deed. If you must be first, be first in prayer–leaving the rest and going a step farther just to pray.

What really counts is with whom you want to be "first." Be first, but not with man. Be first with God. The eternal thinks of it this way: "Whoever would be great among you must be your servant, and whoever would be first among you must be slave of all" (Mark 10:43-44). If you strive to be first before the world, you will remain childish. If you strive to be first with the Eternal, you will put away childish ways and find the man beyond the child within you. "For the Son of man also came not to be served but to serve" (Mark 10:45).

Neglect

> *Why dost thou stand afar off, O Lord?*
> *Why dost thou hide theyself in times of trouble?*—Ps. 10:1.

You have felt yourself being neglected. You have felt that God and man have left you and are hiding themselves from you. Why? You are not the first nor the last to possess this mood toward life.

You are being neglected in a difficult situation *because there are healing forces within the situation.* The very environment against which you rebel may hold an answer for you. The early Christians found this to be so. Said Paul, "We rejoice in our sufferings, knowing that suffering produces endurance, and endurance produces character, and character produces hope, and hope does not disappoint us" (Rom. 5:3-5). Christlike graces are born not in heaven, but on earth, in the very situation wherein you believe you are being neglected. Jesus himself became the Christ, the anointed of God, not by living in heaven, but rather by living on earth even through a time when he prayed, saying, "My God, my God, why hast thou forsaken me?" (Matt. 27:46).

You are being neglected in order that *you yourself may think and work and live.* To think clearly and well is not easy. To work in this pressurized society strains you to the breaking point. To live in times like these can be most frustrating. Nevertheless, God stands afar off at certain occasions in your life in order that you may "work out your own salvation with fear and trembling" (Phil. 2:12).

You are being neglected because *God does not choose to sit in your lap.* God does not choose to be accessible without effort, available without your reaching. Just as the choicest minerals are not found on the surface but are discovered only through effort, so it is only when you seek that you find, and only when you knock that doors are opened to you. It is through personal effort while you are feeling neglected that your motives are tested and your basic integrity is probed.

A distinguished doctor, a general practitioner of the old school of medicine, looked back upon his many years of work and then wisely said, "The great majority of human ills tend toward spontaneous recovery." And so they do. There is an ancient story about a man who felt very much neglected by God. He poses the absence of God this way:

> Behold, I go forward, but he is not there;
> and backward, but I cannot perceive him;
> on the left hand I seek him, but I cannot
> behold him;
> I turn to the right hand, but I cannot see him.
> But he knows the way that I take;
> when he has tried me, I shall come forth as
> gold—Job 23:8-10.

Job looked for God all day, but couldn't find him! Yet he knew and understood that this was a part of life to help him reach the more within him–the security from above.

The Shell

> *Rekindle the gift of God that is within you*—II Tim. 1:6.

Have you ever felt like a chick inside the eggshell? Inside the shell the chick is utterly alone, without food, without outside help of any kind. The chick, without advice from anyone, yields to the natural impulse to peck its way out of the shell. Soon it is in a new world, a world of "others," a world where food is plentiful. The chick reaches the new world simply by claiming the natural gift it already has to peck its way out of a stifling situation.

There are natural gifts you possess—use them. You need not wait for the outside world to free you when you sense that you are in a kind of prohibiting shell. Do not feel insufficient. Do not be afraid to use what you have. Just because you have never before exercised your talents is no reason to assume that you have none. You have gifts—use them.

It is possible to *turn a shell into life—by breaking it up from the inside!* Break through your own ideas of self-limitation. You are the only one who says "I can't." Others have confidence in you. Why not have confidence in yourself? Your defeatism comes from within you. You alone decide how you will act. Break through your own frustrations that have become like a shell around you. The chick can do it and so can you.

Security from Above

The shell around you may be there to *give you some exercise you need.* To just fold your hands and be resigned to the shell is to refuse the life you possess. Exercise yourself. In so doing you will gain the strength you need. The first few pecks the chick makes may create no difference in the shell because the first few pecks may be weak. But gradually, just by pecking away, the chick gains strength and soon finds itself in a new world.

"I remind you," writes Paul to Timothy, "to rekindle the gift of God that is within you." That gift of God is not timidity and more timidity, but life and more life. That gift of God is not weakness and more weakness but a spirit of power and more power. Use the gift of God within you and get out of the shell around you.

The Greatest

Whoever would be great—Matt. 20:26.

You have the biggest job in the world—not the President of the United States, not the Prime Minister of Britain, not the Pope, not the president of the Council of Bishops—but you. You have the biggest job in the world, if you have a sense of helpfulness, a willingness to serve.

A certain woman came to Jesus to consult him about very important jobs for her two sons. The world's biggest jobs to this woman were the positions at the top or close to the top—the places of authority where a person could be seen and would have a good title. Jesus answered the mother of Zebedee's children (Matt. 20:20-28) by insisting that the most important jobs are at the bottom of the industrial scale, the social whirl, the educational level, the work of the Kingdom. On another occasion Jesus pointed out the same truth when he said that the greatest individuals in the kingdom of God were children, not presidents, nor prime ministers, nor popes, nor saints, nor bishops. The top level industrial leaders, the socially elite, the higher educators—these seldom, if ever, think of children. Chief executives and university professors seldom, if ever, have the mind of a child, the childlike approach to life.

So then if you want to have and keep life's most important job, you will have to work *down* to it. Thus the bank president would work his way down so that just before retirement he would be the assistant to the teller. In that position he would know a lot more about his bank's customers than he does now. Thus the construction company executive would work his way down until he reached the peak of his profession—a dirt shoveler—that would be good for his waistline. The university chancellor would work his way down so that just before the age of sixty-five he would be an assistant to an assistant instructor, possibly working intimately with students' problems for the first time. Working our way down toward life's biggest jobs would be good for the head (giving us humility), good for the heart (giving us sympathy), and good for the waistline (freeing us from excess fat).

Your ministers just out of seminary would welcome the opportunity to start in as bishops—possibly bringing some really fresh ideas into that office. If they were successful as bishops they would be given more responsible jobs, slowly working toward the highest office in the ministry, that of being a rural pastor on a shoestring salary forty miles from nowhere. There the pastor would be much more sure of his crown in glory than he would as a bishop.

What is life's biggest job anyway? It's the job where living contact with the common people is maintained. It's the job with the most telling human relationships. It's not the secluded, sheltered office from which the common people are barred. It's the job that remembers these words of Jesus: "Whoever would be great among you must be your servant, and whoever would be first among you must be your slave" (Matt. 20:26-27).

A Towel

> *Jesus . . . girded himself with a towel*—John 13:3-4.

Take a towel, please! That's right, just a commonplace towel, even a very unbecoming towel, not necessarily the embroidered kind. Take a towel and use it. Never think of yourself as being above a towel.

There are some very pious souls who believe themselves to be far too saintly for the common chores of life. They prefer to command a situation rather than to serve it. They prefer to give direction rather than to take it. They may have administrative abilities that keep them aloof from the common tasks. They always see to it that they wear the kind of clothing that dictates towels as being out-of-order. So prayer may become an escape for work. So a platform presentation may have more glamour for the "saint" than kitchen drudgery. You don't want to be like that, so please take a towel.

Ideals sometimes strangle themselves through the neglect of practical living. Ideals are good only when they help us to live acceptably day by day. It would be foolish to suppose that we have so much faith that we don't need to work! Faith is good only when it initiates a deed. While faith remains in a cloud, it remains lifeless. Dreams are good only when they do not kill awareness of everyday responsibilities. When dreams blind us to what needs to be done, then our dreams become dead weights. Idealists and dreamers—please take a towel!

But you raise objection! You may not now know how to use a towel, and furthermore, what has that got to do with being a Christian? John said Jesus "rose from supper, laid aside his garments, and girded himself with a towel." Jesus himself took that very unbecoming item called a towel—and he used it. His most intimate friends were present—those who would build his church. So he set them an example. His saintliness was not above the most common task. While he did dream of a better world, he worked at common tasks. His faith was a rugged serviceable part of everyday life. So won't you please join him and take a towel?

Failure

> *Let light shine out of darkness. . . . We are afflicted in every way, but not crushed; perplexed, but not driven to despair; persecuted, but not forsaken; struck down, but not destroyed*—II Cor. 4:6, 8-9.

Your successes bend you to your selfish will. Your failures yield you to the higher unselfish will. Meet life with more of your failures and less of your successes. The breath of life comes from your defeats and not from your victories. Successes blind you; failures give you sight and insight. Failures may help to mature you toward a realization of your own capabilities.

Modesty is a shield hammered out by failure. Humility is an eye which was blind until failure gave it sight. Failure tells you that you are human, and you must know how human you are before you can know how divine you are. Your fear of failure is but a fear of your own humanity.

Failure suggests you be silent; success urges you to shout. In silence you find the peace that failure's lessons would teach you. You know not the depth of your own spirit until you have lost. You know not the degree of your own tenderness until you are defeated. Failure tells you the utter truth about yourself. Before failure came, truth was dead within you. Now it lives. The truth which you would not recognize in success, in failure you embrace.

Let failure come—do not avoid it. Let it lay waste your old dreams, that you may dream anew. Let failure expose your roots and shake them. Let failure kill a part of you, that more of you may live. The cross is a symbol and an experience of addition, not of subtraction. Make it so.

Success has made you hard and cold. Failure may make you warm and tender. In success you love only those who succeeded with you, but in defeat you may love the defeated, the many. In success you may be unforgiving; in failure you may quickly forgive. Failure brings you to the Holy as a beggar saying, "God be merciful to me a sinner." Mercy is only for those who know they have failed—others know not that they need mercy. The merciful have known failure intimately. To be crushed in failure is to release the perfume that was there before but remained unreleased.

Security from Above

Be a student of failure. Be a disciple of the cross. So will you learn that the kingdom of heaven was born anew through darkness, the darkness around a seeming failure called a cross. To you too the Kingdom comes through failure, not success. To you too security comes through a cross, not a crown.

The Seesaw of Life

> *But by the grace of God I am what I am, and his grace toward me was not in vain*—I Cor. 15:10.

In the backyard there was a seesaw for children. One child would sit on one end of the seesaw, the other child on the other end. Then, whenever one child went down, the other youngster would go up. The child with feet on the ground would look up at the other child uncertainly sitting on top with feet dangling.

You are a part of the seesaw system among adults, a system in which you evaluate others and yourself on the basis of whether you are down or up. You falsely assume that your mental and emotional positions must change whenever the physical place or status changes. When the other person goes up and you come down, you do so not only physically but mentally and emotionally. This ought not to be so.

Your position on the seesaw does not change you inwardly. If someone does something better than you do, that does not in any way belittle your talents. You have precisely the same skills as you had before—no more and no less. The other's exceptional skills do not devaluate yours. Your skills do not affect his. And yet, you do think of yourself at times on this false relativistic basis. When you do think this way, remember the children on the seesaw and recall that whether they were up or down had no bearing at all on their capabilities.

Your brother may be richer than you are, but that does not make you feel poorer. Another person may be better looking than you are, but that does not make you feel ugly. Someone may conduct a meeting with great statesmanship, but that does not make you less of a personal counsellor. Another may have greater word-managing skills than you do, but that does not make you tongue-tied. Your position on the seesaw of life does not change "you"—in the eyes of some individuals it may, but actually it cannot change you. So you must not feel mentally or emotionally down because another is up.

Remember that the person who is up on the seesaw of life is in a far more precarious position than the person who is down. The person who is down has his feet on the ground. The person who is up is not sure how long he will be able to stay there. He may enjoy the sensation of looking down at others, but this is an uncertain sensation. He may feel superior at the moment and may seek to make you feel inferior, but remember, without you he would not have gotten up there. In the seesaw of life the person with his feet on the ground is the one who keeps up the other end of the seesaw.

You have a value all your own wherever you may be. You have gifts that are distinctive and unique. Your own writing does not become useless when you read something great in literature such as the Bible. God uses the Bible, but God uses your writing too. So refuse to consider life as an emotional and mental seesaw. Think rather of all of life as having a very important place for each person—for you, and for the other person too. To lose status, to lose a certain position, is never to be equated with losing talents or skills or character. By the grace of God you are what you are. That grace is not in vain. That grace does not change, nor do you really change, wherever you may be on the seesaw of life.

Kicked Upstairs

> *He was lifted up, and a cloud took him out of their sight*—Acts 1:9.

What have they done to you? Have they taken life's calling from you because they thought you were not doing so well? You were not openly dismissed, just quietly set aside and kicked upstairs.

You knew that the congratulations extended you were really condolences. You were expendable and it hurt. You did your best, but the pressure was on and those in power had their way. You had been a pioneer in your field and everyone knew it. Old pioneers never die, they are just set aside and kicked upstairs.

You were told "a larger opportunity," "a greater service," and "an award" awaited you. But you knew that in their language "a larger opportunity" meant retirement, "a greater service" denoted diplomatic doubletalk, and "an award" meant the kiss of death.

Why ever quarrel with the rulers of this world? They have their strategies and their politics. Agree with them, agree at least in the simple fact that there is an upstairs to go to. Maybe not the kind of upstairs they think of, but something profoundly better.

Remember there was a man long ago whose most trusted friends thought he was not doing so well at his job. They had other ideas as to how it ought to be done. They wanted a popular program with a high rating and a majority audience. But he stood for what was true and the truth is never popular. So, they set him aside and gave him a new, high sounding title, "The King of the Jews." They nailed this title on the door of his office. His office was on a hill with three crosses, and one of the crosses was for him.

They had kicked him upstairs better than they

knew. They thought that now he was completely out of the way and his ideas would no longer prevail. He went upstairs—all the way upstairs to the right hand of the throne of God.

He is doing quite well upstairs, thank you!

Love

Love

Love never ends—I Cor. 13:8.

Love ever reminds you that you are a body. Love sometimes tells you that you are a living soul.

Love has many voices–male and female, bold and timid, young and old, rich and poor. When love calls, you follow. When love speaks, you believe. Yet the voices of love may pierce your hope and lay waste your ambition. Be aware of the voices of love. You think your love may buy another's love, but it may only be your need bribing another, and so losing more.

Love may lift you just to nail you to a cross. Love may make keen every sense just to expose you before those you love. Love may burn you with pain and mock you in nakedness toward a firm maturity. All this love may do to you to find you a fitting place in the Kingdom.

You are afraid of love and of what it may do to you and for you. So you seek only the face of love, the form of love—not its heart. You want only love's laughter, not its tears. Love beckons you to the hills of God, but you choose the green valleys. In the valleys you remain afraid of love, forgetting that true love shelters no fear.

Love has desires to make itself fully aware. The desires of love wake in you the supreme consciousness that you are a body. The desires of love crowd the soul until it is as if the soul were no more—the body is aware only of itself. When the body finds release in love and spends itself fully, *then* it is as if the body were no more. At this moment the soul emerges into its own—you know *then* that you are a living soul. "Love never ends."

When your body has parted with all that it has and worn itself out with effort to love, then your soul comes into its own. When your body loses its identity in love, your soul is all and in all. As your body relaxes in emptiness, your soul may be filled with a knowledge of what it is. While your body goes to sleep in exhaustion, your soul wakes and looks forward to another day of loving. Love ever reminds you that you are a body. Love sometimes tells you that you are a living soul, that you are more.

"Love never ends."

Marital Love

For this reason . . .—Matt. 19:5.

"My husband makes me so mad sometimes that I could pick him up by the seat of his pants and throw him out of the window. But then *I* would be the first one to go out and pick him up again!" This is a way of love that is amusing and yet meaningful.

To love a person in marriage is not to suggest complete agreement in everything, but rather to know that there will be disagreements. And yet the disagreements will be understood in love so that they will not end in disagreeableness. The temptation may be present to physically harm the other, but immediately there will be the reaction to be sorry and to come to the rescue.

Jesus said, "He who made them from the beginning made them male and female, and said, '*For this reason* a man shall leave his father and mother and be joined to his wife, and the two shall become one' " (Matt. 19:4-5). The accent is on being together, not becoming alike. In marriage each is to maintain his maleness and her femaleness. Each will still see and know life through his or her own eyes, background, education, sex. The man is not to become like the woman, nor the woman like the man. Male and female cannot possibly be completely one in thought and deed—ever! Throughout life they are still uniquely male and uniquely female, maintaining some differences of outlook and opinion, but maintaining these differences in love. "For this reason"—because they are different each from the other: male and female—they choose to live together.

Marital love at its best is not to seek to tolerate the differences that come, but rather to seek to understand them. To just endure each other through conflicting opinions is sooner or later to allow love to die. In affection to find the reason for the differences, to learn "why," is to keep love alive. Then, when in a trying moment one wants to throw the other out of the window, there will also be the realization that one would be the very first to come to the rescue—because love is really there—all the time.

Love basically wants the other to be different—to be male or female—the choice was made "For this reason. . . ."

Parenthood

Our Father who art in heaven—Matt. 6:9.

Do not boast that you are altogether the father of your child. God is much more the father of your child than you are. You have no power to create a body and a mind like that of your child. Your role in fatherhood is subordinate to that of the Father above. Your child is not exclusively your child. Your child is the child of life.

Measure your child by the ages that are past and the ages that are to come. This offspring comes to give you wisdom. This young person seeks to show you the meaning of more. If your life is in quest of life, go search for it in your child. There is no grave within this young heart. Here is your strongest link in the chain of eternity. Here is the truth in full strength. Here is the ancient of days sitting in your lap.

Bless your child for giving you much and yet not knowing that he is giving you anything. Bless your child for possessing a love that will not let you go and yet not knowing that this is love. Bless your child for being true to himself without ever being aware of it. Bless your child for believing without seeing in a world that will not believe unless it sees. Bless your child, for of such is the kingdom of heaven.

Here is the stranger at your gate. Keep him, but not as a stranger. Show the true way for this little one through the early years of beginnings that through earth's endings the Father above may find this child to be truly his. Do not keep your child as a stranger.

Through your child live toward forever, that your child may not live for time alone. Guard not only the entrances but also the exits of this new life in your keeping. This child is your father and mother; this child is the continuing of your generations to come. Fulfill the life of your child by making real to him the life of your Father in heaven. Lead your child to look for two fathers in heaven—you and your heavenly Father.

Here in your child is the story of life told in innocence, set in holiness, disclosed in tenderness. Be the father your Father expects you to be. Be *more* than you are. Share your security with your child and let your child give you of the security he possesses.

Death or Distance

Husbands, love your wives—Eph. 5:25.

Death can part us and so can distance!

During the days of slavery, whenever slaves were married an additional phrase was included in the ceremony. The slave preacher uniting the slaves in marriage would add "until death or distance do you part." Many were the partings by distance when families were broken up—a man sold to one master, his wife to another. When this happened, the couple was considered divorced. They recognized death and distance as parting factors.

"Until death or distance do you part" ought to be included as a part of every wedding ceremony. Distance does separate. Distance can take the heart out of a wholesome love. Love can be at its best only when it has continuing opportunity to express itself at close range. If the hungers of love remain unsatisfied because of distance, love may starve itself to death. "Until death or distance do you part" is no idle phrase. It is not only meaningful for the slaves of a generation past, but also it is pertinent for the free men and women of today.

The job a man holds, a woman's professional drive, the crisis of age—all these may separate lovers until the love cools and dies. Like the slaves of a past century, we too may have no choice. We try to bear up bravely under the pressures of new separating experiences. The job has its demands, the professional career calls us, age leaves no alternative. The miles that are between us become tempting miles. The hunger for affection is keen but there is no satisfaction for it. Distance, like death, does its deadly work and we find ourselves its victims.

There are other distances that separate—not the distances of miles but the distances of indifference and neglect. Failure to appreciate each other can create a sense of distance that only a revival of love can overcome. Time itself may become a separating factor, like distance. The years come and go, and sometimes love too comes and goes with the years. Each grows apart from the other until two good people are no longer good for each other.

The New Testament has a verse in it that applies here. It says, "Husbands love your wives, as Christ loved the church and gave himself up for her" (Eph.

5:25). Christ loved through the difficulties of time and space. Distance had its temptations for him too. The church was not all in a huddle close to him. The church, as it is today, as we know it, was far, far away in time and in miles and in growth for him. Yet he loved it and gave himself for it. There is our ideal—to live so wisely and so well that distance will never take love from us.

Divorce Houses

> *No city or house divided against itself will stand*—Matt. 12:25.

What are "divorce houses"? You will find them on the island of Barbados in the West Indies. When a divorce is granted to a native Negro couple, all possessions are divided equally. Everything is divided as evenly as possible. Sometimes the husband will even saw the family house in two and then take his half away with him. The open sides of the sawed-up house are boarded up. Then these structures are known as "divorce houses"—houses that have been sawed in two as the result of divorce.

"Divorce houses" *are not peculiar to the island of Barbados.* They are native to every country in the world. It is true that the sawed-up structure may be distinctive to the West Indies, but the "divorce house" and the divided house may be found the world over. Jesus thought of it when he said, "No city or house divided against itself will stand."

There is the divided house that *comes to a couple*—a man and a woman who were once happily married but now decide to call it quits. Both begin to saw away at the separation, dividing all their possessions as equally as they can. But the foundation of the home does not yield easily to the saw—foundations are built of solid stuff. It is most difficult to divide a foundation. Division does not quite solve all the problems it was hoped it would solve. The divided house finds it hard to stand.

There is another type of divided house that involves another couple—*God and man.* A most happy relationship existed at one time. Spiritual experiences of love and devotion were common. Good cheer was the order of the day. Peace of mind and of heart was the usual thing. A sense of security for the here and the hereafter had become a habit of life. Fellowship with the Eternal was a daily event. Then something happened. Perhaps an unanswered prayer. Maybe an unfortunate tragedy. A loss keenly felt. God was blamed. God was shunned. God was set aside. A divorce was willed. The house of the human spirit was divided. Happiness is sought now, but not found. Peace, security, and fellowship have become only memories. The divided house finds it hard to stand.

"Divorce houses!" *Bring them together again.* Houses were never meant to be sawed in half. Foundations of love and faith and hope were intended for united, not divided, houses. A man and a woman once happily married can find happiness again in each other. Your own relationship with God himself, once so wholesome and enjoyable, can be that way again. Bring the sawed-up "divorce houses" together again. You can do it. You can.

Hate

> *No one can serve two masters; for either he will hate the one and love the other, or he will be devoted to the one and despise the other*—Matt. 6:24.

There is a narrow road between love and hate. Love may turn to hate quickly, but hate may not easily love again. The road between love and hate is straight and narrow; the traffic upon it is swift—there is no parking.

Your hate is caught between yesterday and tomorrow. It is hard to go back into yesterday and you know not how to go into tomorrow. Your hate can tell you many things about yourself.

Your hate tells you how little you are, how primitive you can be. Your hate may shrink you so that where you once were great, you are now small. Your hate may turn a life into a moment, and a moment into a life. The more you hate, the less you will live. Hate will tell you that faith is vain and hope is futile. Hate will lie to you, steal from you, imprison you, take away your heart. Hate lays waste. Hate can communicate nothing but hate.

Hate is your enemy. Know this and you will seek until you find the narrow road back to love again. Remember that the road is narrow, just wide enough for faith and hope but nought else beside. The road goes straight uphill, demanding all your strength and courage. Spend yourself to reach it and it will make life livable again.

The love that has come back out of hate is a different love. It now knows more than love needs to know. It now needs more forgetting and more remembering —more forgetting the yesterdays and more remembering the possibilities of the tomorrows. It now needs to be ever loving, that it may never be tempted to hate again.

Hate that has known love and then lost love hates all the more. Love that has known hate and has overcome it seeks to love with all heart, all mind, all strength. The fullness of love overcomes all suggestions to hate again. Perfect love blocks the narrow road that leads to hate and goes on its way to abundant life—to the more within.

Loneliness

> *I lie awake,*
> *I am like a lonely bird on the housetop*—Ps. 102:7.

You say that you are wanted only for your smaller self that walks with the crowd. You say you are not wanted for your most real self. You are wanted only for your position, your means, your prestige. You remain unwanted for your true being. You are wanted in public life but unwanted in your private life. Where you are most hungry, there you find no food. The mansion of your most real being has a door that remains shut and a window with blinds drawn. You are alone.

Time has changed your wants. Years ago you wanted most to be wanted by the crowd; now you want to be wanted supremely for your basic self. You want to be wanted for what you really are, not for what you are on parade. Age has sifted your wants until only the most basic are left. To be wanted by everybody is to be wanted for the superficial part of you. So you remain alone.

There is somebody who wants you. The dignity you have built up through the years has become a wall preventing that somebody from reaching you. Your public life has made you forbidding to the one who wants you. So you face blank walls and naked ceilings through your lonely nights. The glory of your days makes more real the tragedy of darkness when the night comes. Your mind is empty while your body is full. Yet there is somebody who wants you.

Your delight is winning crowds to your thinking, but you cannot seem to win one person to your basic self. You wear the crowd as a yoke and a handcuff. Do not give up the crowd, lest you lose your calling. Commend your spirit, the spirit that wins the crowd—commend it to God who gave it to you. But to whom will you commend your hungry body? Who will deliver you from your most needy self? A good Samaritan may. An understanding angel may. Time alone may. Death will.

Do not worship your status. Do not bow in reverence before your place in the crowd. Beware of your talents and your skills—they may betray you. To remain unwanted is to live at a dying rate. It is to become a fragile part of your full self. Acknowledge your loneliness. Open your life to Life. Your whole being needs to be satisfied until your nights become as days. Where you are most hungry, you can be fed. The powers of which you are capable are needed by someone. Open your eyes, open your ears, open your heart, open your body. You need not remain unwanted. Be found by someone and so become *more*, much more than you now are.

Night

> *Day to day pours forth speech, and night to night declares knowledge*—Ps. 19:2.

Into the night your deepest self goes—enclosed by darkness, uncovered, naked, alone. The night takes others away and leaves you with yourself.

Your eyes are useless now. Your ears hear only the

strange undefined noises coming from nowhere. Your voice creates only an echo of itself through the night. The night neither sees, nor hears, nor speaks. You can sense only yourself.

Through the night the coward and the hero play tag within you. The slave and the master mock each other in your wakefulness. The past and the future challenge the dark present to bring some flame into the night, but there is no flame, no light.

The night hides you, but you do not want to hide. You feel for yourself without eyes or ears or voice, but your own feelings were not meant for you—they were meant for another.

The night brings you what was left of a wretched day. The crumbling leftovers you take into the darkness, and the leftovers only blacken the darkness.

What can you do with the night? The child ignores it and sleeps in peace. The tired laborer, having used his flesh and muscles through the day, relaxes and sleeps as the child. But you who have used your mind through the day cannot stop the mind when the night comes. Day and night are alike to the higher self.

What can you do with the night? You can reach with the fingertips of your soul for the love that will not let you go. The night knows no time, no space. Remember to remember that spirit with Spirit may meet; the darkness upon the face of the deep may close its eyes and find inner light.

In the beginning the light was separated from the darkness (Gen. 1:4). Every night needs a beginning like that. The separation comes when you learn that darkness was meant to be on the outside only; the night was meant to surround you and not to get inside you. Let there be light through the night inside you. So will you sleep as the child–trustfully, hopefully, lovingly, securely.

Meet Yourself

> *The kingdom of God is in the midst of you*—Luke 17:21.

The source of all the worst and all the best lies within you. Most of your troubles and most of your joys are self-caused. The little boy was right when he said to his mother, "Everything I do you blame on me!" The little boy was just meeting himself.

If you are unhappy it may be that there is something wrong within you. Do not blame the outer world, but rather look to the inner world within you. Your difficulty may be loneliness, or a wayward child, or a wandering husband or wife, or a financial crisis. Whatever there may be that is wrong, look within you and meet yourself.

Perhaps your attitudes have been vengeful, condemnatory, or selfish. These inner attitudes may have created the outer situation you dislike so very much. Your sensitive moods may have brought about the indifference you detect in others. Your attitudes toward others may be creating your present unhappiness. Remember that like begets like. When you are unhappy you are just meeting yourself.

If you are a happy person then it may be that you have found that "the kingdom of God is in the midst of you." Your attitudes of love, commendation, and unselfishness have created the beautiful world in which you live and move and have your being. Here again like begets like. When you are happy you are meeting yourself.

You are happy because you know God is and that you are a part of him. You are happy because you know life has purpose and meaning. You know that love does many things for you that nothing else can do. You know that love is fulfilling. You are aware that your own will creates your own destiny. You have studied yourself and come to know that the answer to most of your problems lies within yourself—not within your neighbor, your doctor, your pastor, nor anyone else.

Because you are willing to tackle life within yourself and not run away, you have met God's kingdom and it is yours to have and to hold through life and death and life again.

Won't you rejoin God in his plan for your life and in so doing find that "the kingdom of God is in the midst of you"? Then whatever you do, you will meet yourself—your best self.

Your Measurements

> *To the measure of the stature of the fulness of Christ*—Eph. 4:13.

What are your measurements? There are some of your own personal measurements that can be given you. Your mouth, your ears, and your nose are all of equal length. The middle joint of your small finger is half the distance of your lips. Your eyes are half the length of either your ears, your nose, or your mouth. These are your own personal measurements that can be given you.

Generally, we may give you other measurements too. By using the eye as a unit of measurement, your face is five eyes wide. The area between your eyes is one eye wide. The base of your nose is one eye wide. Your mouth is two eyes wide. Your ear is two eyes high. Your nose is two eyes high. These measurements go back to Egyptian times, but are still used by artists today. There are other measurements you alone can give.

What are the measurements of your *faith?* Jesus spoke of those who had "little faith" (Luke 12:28). Then there were others whose faith measurements were nil. Of them he said, "Why are you afraid? Have you no faith?" (Mark 4:40). What are the measurements of *your* faith?

What are the measurements of your *love?* Of a certain woman the Master said, "Her sins, which are many, are forgiven, for she loved much; but he who is forgiven little, loves little" (Luke 7:47). Does what you say with your life about love measure the same as what you have heard about love with your ears?

What are the measurements of your *future?* Can you see only as far as the end of your nose? How extensive are your life plans? Does your measurement of the future end abruptly with the grave or does it go beyond that? Does your future find itself enclosed among the boundaries of about seventy years, maybe a little more, maybe a little less? What are the measurements of your future?

An ancient writer had this hope for you. He said it was his hope that you would "Attain to the unity of the faith and of the knowledge of the Son of God, to mature manhood, to the measure of the stature of the fullness of Christ" (Eph. 4:13). Your faith should move in the realm of greatness. Your love could be expansive enough to be willing to "lay down its life for its friends." The forgiveness issuing from that love could be boundless. The future could have a quality of everlastingness about it. May your measurements seek to match the "measure of the stature of the fulness of Christ."

Body

Body

> *But I, brethren, could not address you as spiritual men, but as men of the flesh*—I Cor. 3:1.

You never asked for your body, but your body keeps forever asking, raising all kinds of questions about itself. Your desires are the askings of your body. You are a man of the flesh.

The answers you give to the questions your body raises—these have a time to live and a time to die. Do not try to give your body today's answer to yesterday's question. As the askings of your body change from day to day, so must the answers to these askings suit the day and not the yesterday.

Your body helped to create the lives of your children. In their bodies you see your body, but only a part. They have of the old, but they are new. They are like you, but yet different from you. They bear only the image of your body through a little of its substance.

Your body is your dictator. It tells you what to do and when—and you do it. Where your body leads, you follow. Others know your body, but you find difficulty in knowing it yourself. The body has a language all its own, punctuated with laughter, sighs, pain, growth, deterioration.

The scales tell you your weight, but your weight tells you nothing. You know how tall you are, but so many feet and so many inches tell you nothing. There are some who will flatter you by telling you how handsome or how beautiful you are. Do not take the measurements nor the comments of others seriously. The weight, height, appearance of your body—these tell you nothing. To be guided by these criteria is to be ultimately deceived.

The body will reach a stage where it can no longer support itself fully. The eyes need glasses, the ears need a hearing aid, the feet need arch supports, the face needs more and more cosmetics. Your body is the temporary house you live in. Through pain and age you become aware of a temporary housing problem.

Who will support the body at the last in full? No one . . . *no one.* It will be carried to a grave with pomp and ceremony. It will be placed in the ground. It will be covered. Your body will be forgotten while a new generation remembers only itself. Your body will rest in the earth. You will know then that you are more, much more than your body—you are a living soul, and your security lies *not* in your body but your soul.

Punishment

> *We know that in everything God works for good with those who love him, who are called according to his purpose*—Rom. 8:28.

You were punished when you were a child, but now that you are a man you feel you are beyond punishment. Much in you is still a child and ever so much in you has not yet become a man.

The child within you thinks that the wrong you do is done only to others. The child within you exempts itself from wrong. The man you can be knows that the wrong you do is done not only to others but to yourself as well. Wrong is not only objective, but subjective too. The wrong you do cannot be kept a stranger to you. You are accountable. You live with yourself—with the just and the unjust.

You will survive all the punishment you need that will be given you. Your body can take it, and so can you. Your body can do without tonsils, appendix, gall bladder, spleen, one of two kidneys, one of two lungs. Your body can survive even if two of your four or five quarts of blood are drained from you. Even if most of your stomach is cut out, you can live. Should four of the twenty-three feet of your small intestine be removed, or should half of your brain be taken from you —you could survive. All this physical, bodily punishment may not kill you. Your body is rugged and so are you.

You will live and survive all the punishment your soul may need. Sorrow may smite you. Loneliness may gnaw at your heart. Age may first whisper and then shout your frailties—but you will live. You may be snubbed, denied, forgotten twenty-four hours each day—but you will live. You may be blessed in reverse by your friends and haunted by your relatives. All you possess may be taken from you, but still you will live.

Your soul will survive all the punishment given it. When your personal world comes tumbling down before you, you will take the shoes from your feet and know that you are on holy ground. The darkness that comes with your crucifixion will not last. You will be taken down from your cross. Your best friends will bury you, but you will not remain buried. You will live. Your soul can take it.

Then you will live as you have never lived before.

Closed doors will be no barrier to you. Time will not limit you. The new person you will be will be punished no more. You will live and live and *live* toward the *more* that you are.

An Itching Nose

He put them into the inner prison—Acts 16:24.

Promptly at eight o'clock each evening for six full weeks the patient had to be placed in an iron lung. He would remain in the iron lung until seven each morning with only his head exposed. All night long his entire body was sealed in, so that the iron lung could breathe for him to give him the air and the rest he needed. When asked what his biggest problem was during these long nights in iron, he said: "My biggest problem was that when my nose itched I had no way of scratching it!"

So many of our lives are problem-centered. We think of the "iron lungs" in which circumstances have placed us. The protective armor that conditions our existence is something we rebel against because we want to be free. Life has "locked us in" and we resent the locks. Here was a man in an iron lung whose biggest problem was not the hard casing around him, but just an itching nose and no way to scratch it.

Sometimes it is the little irritation close to the really big problem that annoys us most. Attention is fixed not upon the whole body that finds it difficult to get air but upon a little piece of skin that teases us to be scratched. Little things become big and big things shrink in size when our patience is tested. An item of little consequence keeps us awake in the prison house of fate. A small fraction of our being annoys the whole being, if we let it be so.

You there, in an "iron lung" not of your choosing, with "an itching nose" to add to it, what can you do? You can rebel and so make yourself still more uncomfortable. You can let the "iron lung" breathe for you and give your body what it needs. Inflexible conditions like iron lungs, are not necessarily there to hurt us. They may be there to help us. For the extra of "an itching nose" you can ask the nurse standing by to scratch it for you! She won't mind. There is someone usually around to take care of the little thing that bothers so much. When life hems you in, restricts you, prevents you from taking care of the little things, then face the little annoyance that has become big and if you cannot find relief—accept it smilingly.

Wherever, However, Whoever

Whenever you will, you can do good—Mark 14:7.

They were two clean-looking, bright-eyed teen-agers—a boy and a girl. The elevator door had opened for a moment on the sixth floor of the hospital, and there they were. The boy was flat on his stomach on the kind of a carriage used to take patients to the operating room. His head was lifted in animated conversation, his eyes fastened on the attractive girl before him. She was in a wheelchair, hospitalized as he was, and yet radiating life as she talked in exciting ways to him. Each ignored the other's physical condition. Each forgot all the physical discomfort, because interest in the real other was more meaningful. And then the elevator door closed upon that arresting unforgettable sight.

Does it matter so much *where* you are when you meet people and are interested in them? You may prefer to meet another in a school, at a party, in a home. But if life puts you in a hospital flat upon your stomach or in a wheelchair—even there you may meet some of the nicest people. At a party your appearance counts for more than it is worth, but in a hospital, dress doesn't matter; appearance hardly counts. Each looks into the other's spirit and sees a friend.

Does it matter so much *how* you are physically? It is the spirit that counts. What the boy's physical difficulty was did not matter. What possible disease or accident the girl had did not matter. But this did matter: They really didn't care about their conditions. Each saw the real other—not the other's infirmity—but the other! Each saw the light within, not the shadows without. Each saw the possible future, not the distracting present. Youth looked at youth and was interested and hopeful.

Security from Above

Does it matter so much *who* you are socially? He may have come from the other side of the tracks. She may have been one of the coming season's debutantes. But here on a hospital carriage or in a wheelchair it made no difference. Appearances sometimes are deceiving. The boy looked deeply into her spirit, and she into his, and they were happy. They were not concerned about each other's status out in the world.

And so, what does this have to do with you now? Just this: *Wherever* you are, *however,* you are, and *whoever* you are there is somebody of interest to you. Lift up your head. Open your eyes, smile away from your troubles and notice how quickly you will meet another smile radiating faith, hope, love through a troubled world.

Wrong Number

> *Increase our faith*—Luke 17:5.

The patient had a story to tell. He was married for the first time when he was seventy years old. He had been married for six years. He was hospitalized and had come through an operation. He said that the day after the operation the phone rang at home at five o'clock in the morning. His wife jumped out of bed and said to herself, "He is dead, and they are calling to tell me!" She got to the phone, answered it, and found out that someone had dialed the wrong number!

As the man told the story, he was reminded of life's repeated experiences with "wrong numbers."

It is easy to jump to conclusions. What else could a phone call at five in the morning mean, but that death had come? But it was the wrong jump to the wrong conclusion. The mind has a way of making snap judgments because it takes time and patience to get at the truth. The ring of the phone meant absolutely nothing until the receiver was taken off and the voice at the other end had a chance to say what it was ready to say. Conclusions were out of order then and are now. We must wait until all the facts are in—always. It may be just a "wrong number."

It is usual to relate one event to another, whereas they may be totally unrelated. The ringing of the phone had nothing at all to do with the husband in the hospital, but the mind was quick to relate where there was no relationship at all. One and one make two only if they are of the same kind: one apple and one hammer does not make two of anything. Each event, each kind must stand by itself until relationship (if any) is known and understood. Otherwise it is the "wrong number."

It is common to expect the worst rather than the best, whereas the best is just as likely to occur as the worst—even if the patient is seventy-six years old! The best did occur. He did recover from the operation. He did live. He did get back home safe and sound. To expect the worst was just to accept the "wrong number." Life is geared to the side of faith, unless you change gears. You do believe, but your belief may be asleep early in the day. Faith is the order of the day even at five o'clock in the morning. Believe the best. The worst may be the "wrong number."

Faith Healing Discontinued

Who heals all your diseases—Ps. 103:3.

On the Saturday church page in a certain newspaper appeared this ad: "Faith healing will be discontinued this week due to the illness of the pastor."

There is a kind of faith healing that is interrupted by the illness of the pastor. There is another kind of faith healing that is never disturbed by the illness of others, not even the pastor. You who are ill, listen!

Know that God is interested in your recovery. God never leaves when his child is in pain. God is compassionate. His love continues through every discomfort of the body. God cares for you. God's care does not depend upon your pastor's health or his illness. God himself is interested in your recovery.

Direct your mind and heart toward health. Possess the will to live. In the fullest of confidence look for health. Dwell upon thoughts of faith and high courage. Help yourself with cheerfulness. Find the things that gladden the hours of the day and night. Your pastor's presence or absence does not finally decide the issue. Direct your mind and heart toward health, either way or any way.

Read and reread that which will build up your confidence. Remember that there are many hands, many eyes, many minds working toward your recovery. Depend upon that. Cooperate with all who seek your well-being. God works through all who work for you. Believe that now things are working together for good, your good. God is with you, not against you. He is your Father. You are his child. Read again Psalm 103 which says,

> Bless the Lord, O my soul;
> and all that is within me,
> bless his holy name!
> Bless the Lord, O my soul,
> and forget not all his benefits,
> who forgives all your iniquity,
> who heals all your diseases.

Now remember others who are ill. You help yourself toward health by helping others who are ill. You are not the only sufferer in the world. The effort it takes to speak to the patient in the next bed is a healing effort. The energy it takes to lift a glass of water to the lips of the seriously bedridden is a good exercise away from your own weakness. Perhaps the pastor himself is ill and needs your prayer, your faith, your visit. You might help him enough so that he can continue faith healing next week.

Swaddling Clothes

When I was a child—I Cor. 13:11.

A two and a half year-old girl had a very stormy session with her mother. In anger she went upstairs and soon returned wearing a hat and coat and carrying a suitcase in her little hands. Her mother asked her where she was going. She said, "Away!" Her mother asked, "What have you got in the suitcase?" "Diapers," said the youngster!

There are times when you may want to run away from discipline. The child within you—still in swaddling clothes—resents any intrusion from any outside authority. But the baby's clothes still in your hands ought to remind you that you may not be mature enough to flee from the discipline you sorely need.

There are usually one or two significant ideas by which you live—ideas left over from childhood. It may be hard to identify them from the distant scene, because leftovers are sometimes hard to distinguish in today's world. One sure way to find them is to look into the suitcases for your "runaway" trip, and there will be the garments that will remind you of areas you have not yet learned to control. Some ideas by which you still live are childish ideas.

An ancient writer puts it this way "When I was a child, I spoke like a child, I thought like a child, I reasoned like a child; when I became a man, I gave up childish ways" (I Cor. 13:11). What are some of these childish ways you need to give up? To think that you are always right—that is childish! To think that you by yourself can manage life—that too is childish. To think that you no longer need the protecting care of those who know you best—this too is to play the child.

It is not carrying the thought too far to suggest that you may be trying to face the world with diapers in your hands. To truly be a man is to set aside swaddling clothes. It is to be in full control of the major areas of personal life. It is to yield to the discipline of a heavenly Father who knows you well. "When I was a child . . ." suggests that for you childishness is in the past.

Boots on Backwards

> *Whither shall I go from thy Spirit?*
> *Or whither shall I flee from thy presence?*
> *If I ascend to heaven, thou art there!*
> *If I make my bed in Sheol, thou art there!*—
> Ps. 139:7-8.

A low-slung cowboy was evading a posse in snow in Brooklyn. This cowpoke—three feet tall and weighing 30 pounds—had slipped out of his bunkhouse without his mother knowing it. But the police caught him a block and a half away from home.

The police asked him how old he was. He became tight-lipped. Finally he raised four fingers. At the police station he was given lollipops, hot chocolate, and a hero sandwich. Then he told police how he had put them off his track.

"I put my cowboy boots on backwards," he said.

That is quite an idea—to make others think you are going the opposite way. Just do what is *not* expected of you—go the other way. This is how to get away from it all.

But the whole point is that no matter where you go, which way you go—even if you put your cowboy boots on backwards and tread silently in the snow—you are caught at last. To be sure, lollipops and hot chocolate and a hero sandwich must taste good even in captivity. But nevertheless, your trick has been discovered and you are caught.

Somehow or other a higher Authority knows just about all the tricks you can use. This most usual fact of life was well known back in the centuries. Said the psalmist:

> Whither shall I flee from thy presence?
> If I ascend to heaven, thou art there!
> If I make my bed in Sheol, thou art there!

There is no escaping the higher Power. Whether you are four years old or forty or eighty. Indeed, even if you try to play tricks and put your boots on backwards and tread silently away in the snow—even then you cannot escape God.

A Boy Without a Name

There is a lad here—John 6:9.

One of the world's great stories is about a boy without a name. A crowd of adults had followed the Master up a mountain. No grown-up, not even the disciples, had sense enough to bring some food along. Everybody was hungry. But there was a nameless boy present who had the uncommon sense to bring some food. He didn't have much, but he was willing to share it. Jesus used the boy's possessions to feed the crowd.

The interesting thing is that although most people praise Jesus for the miracle, no one praises the boy who had more sense than the whole crowd put together, including the disciples. Without the nameless lad, Jesus' miracle would have been impossible. Philip, Andrew, Peter—all are recognized and named in the story, but the boy whose foresight made it possible remains without a name.

God bless boys! God bless all adults who are interested in them. As long as there are boys in this country, the nation is secure. As long as there are boys in church, the church will live.

The boy is a bundle of hidden talents. Befriend him. Do not impose your prejudices, hates, worries, and fears upon him. What you say carelessly, he takes seriously. You can't tell by looking at him today what he will be tomorrow.

The boy has a sensitive nature. He knows when his home is not right. A nine-year-old California boy went to Reno, Nevada. He was alone. A policeman questioned him. The boy insisted his purpose in Reno was legitimate. He just wanted to get a divorce from his parents! Boys are sensitive. They know when there's something wrong at home.

Remember that the boy has a growing mind. He is building a memory. You are helping to build that memory. A Scotsman wrote to his former teacher: "I do not know what life or lives may lie before me. But I know this—that to the end of the last of them I shall bear your mark upon me." You are a teacher of boys —even the nameless boys. What are you teaching them? The Apostle Paul remembered a boy who had the privilege of absorbing a rugged faith that was lived before him day by day. Paul wrote a letter to this lad saying, "I am reminded of your sincere faith, a faith that dwelt first in your grandmother Lois and your mother Eunice and now, I am sure, dwells in you" (II Tim. 1:5). Into the growing mind of this boy was built a great faith.

Remember boys today. Boys with or without a name. They are the men of tomorrow, the church fathers of the coming generations, the new body of Christ.

Communication

Communication

> *And the Word became flesh and dwelt among us, full of grace and truth*—John 1:14.

Even before you are heard, you speak. Your appearance communicates for good or ill. What others *see* in you is as important as what others *hear* from you. Do not favor one form of communication over another. Do not say, "I am being judged only by my words." You communicate with what you are altogether.

It is easy for you not to communicate well. Failure

to communicate comes so naturally to us all. Each person has a different frame of reference within and without. Just to be heard is never enough—you must reach the emotions deeply to create a response. Know how you *sound* to others. Know how you *look* to others. Know how you *feel* to others. Otherwise you will not communicate well.

The person or persons to whom you speak become the mirror of effective or ineffective communication. Watch that mirror well. Do not assume that the mirror is at fault when the real fault lies within and about you. Look well to your audience. They will tell you much about yourself. Their attention or inattention becomes the judge of your communication. They may crucify you—and yet, you may have communicated most effectively!

Note well the forms of insecurity you possess when you try to communicate. You may be too tall or too short. Your body may not match the image your voice conveys. Every speaker has some personal intimate block to effective communication. It may be a bald head, heavy glasses, lisping, false teeth, some mannerism—these and other insecurities are there. Be mindful of what your particular insecurity may be and communicate beyond it in faith, in hope, in love. Remember that even the blind and the deaf and the dumb can and do communicate through their insecurities.

Do not believe more in your words than in your deeds. Your words may make no difference at long last, but your deeds will. Give your words the conscience they need—the conscience of your deeds—so will you communicate lastingly. Be sensitive to your tired, worn-out words. Believe more in what you are than in what you say. Words can become a refuge for creative laziness. You communicate best through what you do, through being what you wish to communicate. Words at best can only whisper; deeds may be seen and heard through time and beyond time.

Communicate so as to make a difference in the life around you. This is the final test of communication. So far in your life, what difference have you made? The years you have lived, the decisions you have made—all represent the opportunities you have had to make a difference. How much longer will opportunity come to you?

Perhaps years ago your communication made a difference, but in recent years mounting pressures, fewer and weaker convictions, have made you a person without distinction in communication. You may have become a person attempting to communicate by being "all things to all" and so becoming nothing to yourself and to the world around you.

Bring back again into your life the deeds that communicate with a difference. Let "the Word become flesh" once more—indeed, again and again! Speak before you are heard. Give legs to your ideas—your legs. Let your faith possess the works that will make that faith live. So will you become more than you are, much more. So will you communicate with what you are altogether.

It was said of the great Communicator that "the Word became flesh and dwelt among us, full of grace and truth."

Understanding

> *Are you also still without understanding?*—Matt. 15:16.

Your understanding depends upon your sympathy, your reason, your insight. Your understanding depends upon your knowing what is special, unique, and individual about each person and each situation. You cannot deal with the selected aspects of another and hope to understand—you must consider the total person and the total situation in order to rightly comprehend.

Science can never understand as you can. Science counts on intellectual abstractions and generalizations. Science develops specialists who know much, but only about a fragment of a person or a situation. Science has no educated heart, no sympathy. Science cannot bring the total person together in love—but *you* can.

The reason you so often misunderstand is because you are so selective, fragmentary, and abstract in your approach. To truly understand you must know the inside as well as the outside. To honestly understand is to see a person not only in relationship to yourself, but to see that person independent of you—as that person fully is and might become.

To understand is to comprehensively evaluate that person or situation, or both, as being uniquely different and individual. No two persons, no two situations are exactly alike. The approach to understanding is through an educated heart. Feelings without education may mislead, and yet to overestimate your intuitions may bring you to a false image.

Understanding accepts another person realistically. It is to acknowledge what another person or situation is—good or bad. So to understand is to forgive. Without forgiveness there can be no understanding.

Understanding cannot be manipulated; it just is. Understanding is the very life of human situations, and life is ever different, ever new and old, old and new, ever growing. You cannot make the old new, or the new old.

Who do you want to understand? Set that person apart from yourself and study that individual altogether. Get to know that person inside out and outside in with your head and your heart. So you may sense the other's needs, fears, hopes as that person senses them. So you may appreciate, apprehend, and unselfishly accept that person. So you may love that individual with your mind and your heart specifically. So will you forgive. So will you understand. So will life have and give more meaning to you and for you. Understanding depends upon you.

Reading

He stood up to read—Luke 4:16.

Think of what you do when you read! What happens to your eyes and your mind? Your eyes see some black and white figures on paper. The mind takes these symbols and transforms them into the thoughts of the person who wrote the words. What a miracle that is!

Behind that miracle of reading is a long history of the invention of the alphabet and of writing. But here you are with the writing in front of you. Your eyes move along the lines with regular jumps. Your eyes may fix themselves on certain words momentarily and then move on. Your eyes may move back over the writing as you seek to double check the thought that has been given you. The average person reads about two hundred fifty words a minute. In about a third of a second your mind absorbs more than one word.

While you read you remember what has gone before. So each word depends on the context—on the sentence it is in and on the story of which it is a part. When you reach the end of your reading, you think over what has been written. This is so commonplace that we fail to see a miracle in it. Yet reading is a miracle! In split-second time the eyes have telegraphed groups of words to the mind. Then the mind through memory has kept the words in harmonious relationship so that they make sense.

The miracle of reading! What do you do with this

miracle? You may use this miracle to absorb the funny paper or the comic magazine. You may know how to use the miracle of reading and then refuse to use it. Many individuals do not care to read. But the ability to read is a miracle intended for noble uses. It is good to recognize this to the upbuilding of your character. Jesus used this blessing to great advantage, for the scripture tells us that "he went to the synagogue, as his custom was, on the sabbath day. And he stood up to read." Jesus read and studied to show himself approved of God as being truly his Son. You may share with Jesus this miracle of reading so often taken for granted.

Education

A sower went out to sow his seed—Luke 8:5.

There is much within you that is just half awake. Your teachers can only tap that which is already within. The wise teacher will lead you to discover that which is half awake in your consciousness. To be truly educated is to have come upon the dawn of your own understanding. It is to command your own growth. It is to stretch to your own full stature, like a planted seed.

A seed has life but it remains half alive until it is planted in the ground. Then it absorbs the good around it, appropriating the sun and the rain. The seed takes from its environment above and below and makes it over into a part of itself. What the seed has and what it receives grow along with its growth. Together full maturity comes. The teachers around you cannot give you their knowledge; you must take it and make it something in keeping with the "seed" within you.

The earth exerts a force of gravity upon your body. Exert your own force of gravity to pull toward you what you know you can learn and understand. You stand alone with faculties peculiarly your own. Develop your unique self by pulling to yourself the skills of which you are capable. Be ceaselessly curious.

In your longing to be learned, do not be content just to know—strive to be wise. Temper your knowledge with faith and love—so will your knowledge become wisdom. Invite God into your knowing. When knowledge lives and moves and has its being in the Eternal, then it becomes wisdom. Wisdom is much of you that has been half awake becoming fully awake.

Keep some doors of the mind closed and others open. Keep the doors of the past closed lest you go too far into yourself and die. Keep the doors toward the sky open, that your ideas may become oriented to the real.

Do not look upon death as the end of your education. Death is but another step of instruction, of discipline, of development. Death takes hold of the final half-awake element within you. Your native faculties can go so far, no further. The higher education you seek must truly be higher—it must come from above. Death is *the* great adventure in the process of higher education. You will know the whole truth beyond your half-wakened existence and the whole truth will make you fully free eternally.

Shades of Gray

> *Be careful lest the light in you be darkness*—Luke 11:35.

Jawaharlal Nehru, Prime Minister of India for seventeen years, died May 27, 1964. Adlai E. Stevenson, chief United States delegate to the United Nations gave this tribute: "Pandit Nehru knew better than most that many of life's great decisions are painted not in black and white, but in shades of gray. . . . The hope of the world rests with leaders who have the gift of firmness and of flexibility. Prime Minister Nehru had both. . . . He was one of God's great creations in our time."

This assessment accents what constitutes greatness among leaders today. Greatness is measured in these times by bringing to the top men who can seek and find great decisions in shades of gray. Distinct whites and blacks are assumed to be out of place, quite unrealistic. It is usually a middle-of-the-road policy, negotiation and compromise, attempting to find answers with both "yes" and "no" in them: These are the marks of modern leadership. We forget that life's highways were not built for middle-of-the-road driving! To have no clear right or left, no distinct black or white, to place the hope of the world in the shady middle, to lead in shades of gray is but to lead ultimately to disaster.

Jesus would not have been able to be a successful modern leader. Said Jesus: "Let what you say be simply 'Yes' or 'No'; anything more than this comes from evil" (Matt. 5:37). This judges the modern leader's ability to say "Yes" and "No" at the same time. Jesus thought in terms of light and darkness (not dimness). He talked of heaven or hell (not purgatory). He reminded his listeners of the narrow or the broad way (not the middle of the road). It was life or death (not living at a dying rate). It was right or wrong (not somewhat).

The great decisions Jesus made were painted in black and white, and therein lies the hope of the world. Remember the temptation of Jesus with its simple, positive answers—no doubletalk. Remember the Garden of Gethsemane with its great decision painted in black and white. Remember the trial and the crucifixion of firmness without flexibility. This truly was God's great creation for our time, all time, and eternity.

What about you and shades of gray? The warning of Jesus is this: "Be careful lest the light in you be darkness." He said:

No one after lighting a lamp puts it in a cellar or under a bushel, but on a stand, that those who enter may see the light. Your eye is the lamp of your body; when your eye is sound, your whole body is full of light; but when it is not sound, your body is full of darkness. Therefore be careful lest the light in you be darkness. If then your whole body is full of light, having no part dark, it will be wholly bright, as when a lamp with its rays gives you light (Luke 11:33-36).

Seek not to paint your great decisions in shades of gray, but in black and white—as Jesus did.

Intoxication

> *And do not get drunk with wine, for that is debauchery; but be filled with the Spirit*—Eph. 5:18.

You are at your best when you are intoxicated—*in the right way*. Your temperance may get you nowhere. In your quiet calm you may be looked upon as being already dead. But when you are vigorously excited and have your emotions set free, then your quickened spirit may lead to the achievement of your glowing dream.

Moderation can sooner or later condemn you. An increasing sense of the commonplace may make you common. The restrained way in which you share your convictions may leave you with no convictions to share.

You need a certain excessiveness about you; you need to get away from being helplessly sane. Refuse to be a bore to yourself and to others. Fill the ruts within your life that you may make new tracks toward the future. Become intoxicated with a dream—you may produce a masterpiece!

Be beside yourself, but not with regret. Subject yourself to burning, but don't burn yourself out. Go ahead of your limitations and discover through intoxication what you are really capable of. Do not let the creativity within you die. To live a hushed life is to walk toward the grave.

To be drunk with liquid spirits is to lay waste your enthusiasms. To be filled with the Spirit of the Eternal is to put your enthusiasms to work. Great masterpieces are waiting to be produced by the intoxicated. Mediocrity has its place, but that place is not for you. Do not be content with things as they are.

Reach for the boundless. Open the windows of life. Lift the roof above your soul. Strive not for the *first* heaven, but for the *seventh.* Live abundantly that your joy may be full. Be transformed through your enthusiasms. When your heart pounds as if it might burst, do not stop. Trust yourself with your enthusiasms. Believe in your intoxications.

You are a child of God, not a child of the commonplace. The sun is not lukewarm. The seasons go to extremes. Nature's intoxication is productive. The corn grows tall through the burning sun. The reservoirs are filled from the drenching rain and man no longer thirsts. You are a child of God and a child of nature. Be intoxicated—*in the right way*—toward a masterpiece!

Suffering

> *We rejoice in our sufferings, knowing that suffering produces endurance, and endurance produces character, and character produces hope, and hope does not disappoint us*—Rom. 5:3-5.

Suffering is an art form. To suffer is to know the highest form of communication with the self. Because you have suffered, you understand. Because you have endured specific anguish, you know. Because you have been in pain, you have been in a holy place.

Why are you so concerned to find out why you suffer? It may be because the sins of the fathers are being visited upon you. It may be you suffer because of inherited weaknesses of the flesh or of the mind or both. Or, perhaps you are suffering because of your children. Your own offspring are so much like you were at that age, and so you suffer as you see your worst in your children! Or, you may be suffering because of your present self–you may have recently occasioned the pain that darts through your body or the wound within your soul that will not heal.

Whatever the cause of suffering may be–it is! Just to live is to suffer. Trying experiences are not for the few, but for the many. To be born is to enter the great fraternity; to live is to grow through pain; to die is to know that this is the way of humanity.

You would not be, were it not for suffering. Pain brought you into life. Pain sustains you in life–your own pain or that of others. You know much more about your father, your mother, your children, your self because you have suffered. You know a part of your deepest self because pain has called your attention to it. You have become most aware of these parts of your body that have reminded you of themselves through their knifelike thrusts. Your maturity was not gained through taking a special course of study, but you are mature because you have experienced not only joy and pleasure but injury, loss, frustration, torment.

Brotherhood would be a fluffy word and not the rugged fellowship it is, were it not for suffering. Take all suffering out of love, and this too would be a meaningless word. Suffering gives life and meaning to language. Suffering makes real the unreal.

The highest form of suffering is to suffer for another. The greatest form of love is to suffer to the death, not for one's self but for another. To lay down your life for another is to find the resurrection and the life—and the more than you are.

Remember that suffering is an art form. To suffer is to communicate with the higher self. Suffering helps to create the drama called "life" for you.

The Cross

> *He who does not take his cross and follow me is not worthy of me*—Matt. 10:38.

To think of the cross may be to think of a piece of jewelry. To think of the cross may be to think of the brass piece on the communion table. To think of the cross may be to think of that which graces the top of a church steeple. But none of these are really the cross—they are just reminders of the Cross of Calvary.

Think now about the cross in your own personal life. This is the cross that really matters! The cross in your life is where your Christian faith with its upward reach clashes with the everyday workaday world in which you live. The cross is where the vertical stabs through the horizontal. The cross is where heaven reaches through hell and touches your earthiness to save you.

The cross is God's hope for you, reaching out when the world seeks to level and flatten you and your ideals. The cross is hope breaking through despair, faith breaking through doubt, love breaking through hate. The cross is the breakthrough the prophets dreamed about.

The cross in your life discloses itself at the moment when you are tempted to subtract Christlike ways. At that moment, overcome the temptation, remembering, "For this very reason [to] make every effort to supplement your faith with virtue, and virtue with knowledge, and knowledge with self-control, and self-control with steadfastness, and steadfastness with godliness, and godliness with brotherly affection, and brotherly affection with love" (II Pet. 1:5-7).

The cross is that experience of pain, loneliness, and

defeat in your life which comes, perhaps not through any fault of your own, but for the sake of others.

The cross is that personal involvement which comes when you identify your deepest self with the Way, the Truth, and the Life of Jesus in this present world. The cross involves you with security from above.

Speaking from Crosses

> *They crucified him, and the criminals, one on the right and one on the left*—Luke 23:33.

To have one's speech conditioned by financial "security," independence, and comfort is one thing. To have one's speech conditioned by nakedness, utter dependence, and pain is something else. It is not nearly as important to listen to the superficial mouthings emerging from the easy life as it is to listen to each carefully chosen word coming through pain.

When men on crosses speak, we had better pay attention. On the cross Jesus said, "Father, forgive." On the cross a thief said, "Save yourself and us." On the cross another thief said, "Jesus, remember me."

At times today men speak from positions of so-called "security" and comfort. Political candidates may be men of wealth, well clothed, well housed, well fed. The audiences they reach may be similarly conditioned. Religious leaders too may address their constituents from positions of special privilege, comparative comfort, and well being. Therefore sermons may rarely attract the hungry or the poor or the needy.

The three men on crosses spoke to each other through the most painful agony. Every word was filtered through a tormented body, a thirsting soul, utter loneliness. Their hands and feet were attached to their last "pulpit"—a cross. From outstretched bleeding hands, from bowed heads of weariness, from utter nakedness, they engaged in dialogue.

So to speak is to speak from the depths. The depths may voice forgiveness: "Father, forgive them." Or the cross may but continue the attitude of unrepentant bitterness: "Save yourself and us!" Or from the dry parched lips may come a simple plea for remembrance: "Jesus, remember me." Either way or any way when men on crosses speak, it is wise to listen most carefully.

If *you* have ever spoken from a cross, you will understand. If you have known only a life of false "security" and comfort so far, you will *not* understand. What you said through terrible agonizing pain, or through frightful loneliness, or through abject defeat—that was the most important you. You were then not attempting to reach a crowd to get more votes. You were just trying to reach someone beside you—someone as naked, as lonely, and as much in pain as you were.

What did you say then from your cross? Was it a forgiving word to those around you? Or, was it an unrepentant word, a bitter word, selfishly asking someone else to save you. Or, maybe through your parched lips with all the meaning your condition could give, you said to God, "Remember me."

To whom are you really listening now? Listen to an echo of yourself on your own personal cross. May what you hear yourself say be "Father, forgive" and "Remember me."

A Question

The doors were shut, but Jesus came and stood among them—John 20:26.

Why, O Lord, my Lord,
Why is it that
Only when doors are shut
Dost thou come to me?
Why—*only* when
Doors are shut?

The hard cold door of self-denial,
The clear glass door of indecision,
The swinging door of compromise,
The deeply stained door of frustration,
The folding door of doubt—
All shut *before* Thou dost come to me.

Must eyes be closed
Before I can see?
Must darkness come
Before I find the light?
Must life be empty
Before it can be filled?

Must I retreat
Before I can advance?
Must I die

Before I can live?
Must I be laid in a tomb
Before I can rise again?

O Lord, my Lord
Why is it that
Only when doors are shut
Dost Thou come to me?
Why—*only* when
Doors are shut?

Is it because
The answer
Lies curled up
Within the question?

"The doors were shut, but Jesus came and stood among them."

Truth

Pilate said to him, "What is truth?"—John 18:38.

You do not possess truth. Truth possesses you. If you possessed truth, then truth would be subject to you alone. Truth is greater than you.

You may be the father of new truth; you cannot be its mother. Truth is always being born, and it is mothered by time until the hour of birth. The world may not recognize it, but you will. You will not escape your child.

The truth lies not in what you have heard, but in what you have lived and found to be so. The truth grows and you grow with it. The truth grows faster than you do, and so seems to change, but it is only the change of growth.

Truth lives between the crowd and the solitary way, between the majorities and the minorities.

Let not truth become a conversation piece. Do not make an ornament of it. Truth is a subject for life rather than talk. Judge it not by the moment alone, but by the experiences of the majorities and the minorities, the ages and the moment. Judge truth not by yourself, but toward humanity.

Truth will never lock you in. You cannot imprison truth. Let truth lead you through the wilderness of your confusions to the promised land.

Do not fear if others doubt the truth as you know it. Sufficient to your day and night is the truth it brings.

Do not condemn the truth in others. Others are different from you. The truth in which they live meets their personal needs, as the truth in which you live meets your personal needs. You do not know all the truth, and neither do they. This is for the good of all.

Remember that the truth is never impulsive. It never raises a sword. The truth has no teeth, only a shield. It has no head, only heart. The truth has no lord; it is Lord of all. The truth has no earth, only heaven.

Know the truth, but above all else let the truth know you. In knowing, you let the truth become your

Lord and Master. Lose your life to truth and you will find it again, richer than it ever was before, more secure than it has ever been before.

Justice

> *Love your enemies and pray for those who persecute you, so that you may be sons of your Father who is in heaven; for he makes his sun rise on the evil and on the good, and sends rain on the just and on the unjust*—Matt. 5:44-45.

Life reminds you in subtle ways of the little you possess. Then even the little you have is taken from you. You turn around and observe that those who already have, receive even more. There seems to be no justice.

Life gives and takes away with purpose. Life is not blind. Life gropes not in the dark. Something greater comes when the lesser is taken away. Sometimes the evil is taken from you and sometimes the good. You may not have known the evil as evil or the good as good, unless it was taken from you.

When you are left in emptiness, you see the form of your being more clearly than you could in your fullness. Those who have and so receive the more can never see the true shape of their lives. So the rich find it hard to enter the Kingdom. Riches blind. Wealth belittles. Possessions numb.

Justice will out. Justice is mothered by patience. Justice is not confused by what it sees. Justice grows through what it knows. Justice recognizes the end from the beginning. What seems the end to you is not the end of justice; it is only the beginning. Justice will out at the last.

Life seems to be such a respecter of persons! You have labored but seemingly in vain and others reap in joy what they have not sown. In your poverty you want to damn their luxury. Remember that life is not just three score years and ten. Measure not life by years, but by forever. Measure not justice by this day alone.

Justice dwells within you. Justice is of the spirit and not of the letter. Justice is of the soul and not of the flesh. Justice functions from above and not from below.

Justice lives with truth. Justice is the child of truth. Truth will never deny justice, nor will justice ever leave truth.

Do not hate justice because it seems to be untrue to itself. Love justice. Give justice the opportunities it seeks within you. Justice depends not upon the things that perish, but upon the things that endure. Let ultimate justice bring you spiritual values and bring you to the threshold of your God-given possessions of mind, heart, and soul. So will you know the wisdom of justice toward forever, and toward security from above.

Prayer

Prayer

> *Continue steadfastly in prayer, being watchful in it with thanksgiving*—Col. 4:2.

Prayer is your deepest longing, right or wrong. Prayer is the cry of your soul coming through your body. Prayer is the deepest expression, the highest communication. Prayer is the language universal.

You pray; everyone prays one way or another. Multiplied prayers mean that all life is open to God from many sides. Each person seeks an answer for himself.

To answer one prayer may be to deny another. The self is always within the prayer each creates.

There are prayers that come from your soul. There are prayers that come from your flesh. Look to the source of your prayer. The prayer that comes from your soul is warm and holy. The prayer that comes from your flesh is hot and passionate. There is a prayer that comes from both the soul and the flesh when these cry out for the living God.

Your prayers are answered. Sooner or later your deepest longing is heard. The answer to your prayer may come through the sunshine or through the clouds, through the heat or through the cold, to your face or to your back. But the answer comes and you know it.

Your prayer has its own clock, its own calendar. Standard time, days or weeks have little to do with prayer. Your prayer has its own soul-saving time. Your prayer waits for its moment of fulfillment when your deep longings and the longings of others are resolved without conflict.

Do not give up your prayers. Do not let them go. Nurture your prayers with patience. Lead them through the valley of the shadow of time, that they may not fear.

Look to God through your prayers, and let God look at you through your prayers. Your prayers will tell you much about yourself. The cry of your soul through your body is the echo of what you really are in your deepest self. Come to know the uttermost within you through prayer.

Kneel before your prayers and, having prayed, kneel yet more, until the bending of your body brings an ache to your prayers. Let your knees take away all the superficial, all the unreal about your prayers. Let your prayers come naked before the throne of grace that God may see you as you are, and that you may see yourself as God sees you. So will you become more than you are, and become at one with security from above.

Need

> *When I was a child, I spoke like a child, I thought like a child, I reasoned like a child; when I became a man, I gave up childish ways*—I Cor. 13:11.

You think you know what you need. Why is it then that what you felt you needed ten years ago, you know you do not need now? Your needs remain changeable, fragile, questionable.

Your needs go wandering in the wind, unguarded. Your needs are met and yet your hands are empty. Your needs know you not. They know not how fickle you are. Your needs stand with their backs to God. You live between your needs and God. You live in the shadow of your needs and are hungry.

When you find what you thought you needed, you

may be betrayed. Instead of living with you, the met need will separate itself from you and laugh at your misery. You thought that the need that was met would prove to be a crown. It was a crown—a crown of thorns. What you think you need is always insufficient, imperfect, incapable, fleeting.

What you say you need is not what you really need. The emptiness about you that you seek to fill is deceiving. You need freedom, and then you discover you can only have freedom in the prison of discipline. You need peace of mind, but that comes only through the conflict of many ideas and the defeat or victory of some. You need the felt companionship of another. Then ultimately you find that your best companion is your unseen Friend. You accept him and "see" him only in faith. The hope that endures emerges through the ashes of yesterday and tomorrow.

When occasionally you get what you need, you find it is not what you thought it was. It does not do what you thought it would do for you. You embrace the answer to your need and find the answer is only a question. Answers are sometimes questions curled and shrunk within themselves, like this: ?

Forget your own needs—remember the needs of others. Stand aside from your own hungers and beside the hungers of others. Feed another and you feed yourself best. Set aside your needs and you save your life. Meet your own needs and you lose your life. You do not really know what you need. You are more, much more than what you think you need.

Now

> *The appointed time has grown very short*—I Cor. 7:29.

Time is shrinking for each of us. There is not as much time left today as there was yesterday. Our "appointed time has grown very short." So what?

Think of the petty things that embitter your heart. Think of the quarrel that has separated you from another. Think of the jealousy that boils within you. Think of the stubborn pride that refuses to face reality. Time is shrinking for you. Only now is left.

Why keep all these annoyances alive? Why continue to feed them at such great cost to yourself? Why allow a spite to continue when the person who is the object of your spite may be dead tomorrow? Why not break the spell now and stop worrying your heart and your face?

Speak the forgiving word now. Yield your mind to tolerance and understanding now. Open your stubborn heart to sympathy and kindness now. Remember that "the appointed time has grown very short."

Now is the time. There may never be another time, nor a better time. Smile now and greet the person you have avoided in the immediate past. Forgive and forget—just as you expect to be forgiven and have others forget your shortcomings.

Time is shrinking. This earthly life is too short for vengeance and malice. See virtues in others as you hope others may see virtues in you. You may be a "graduate nurse" in the area of nursing your wounds. Stop it now.

The most favorable circumstances for loving your enemy will be found in the present. Tomorrow never comes. "The appointed time has grown short." Now is here. Forgive. Forget. You will feel happier and so much more at peace with yourself with malice toward none and love for all—*now.*

After Prayer?

> *A faith that dwelt first in your grandmother Lois* —II Tim. 1:5.

"This I ask for Jesus' sake. Amen. *Now* give me my candy." This was the strange conclusion to prayer a little three-year-old girl made. It seems that her father was anxious to record her voice. So he taught her to say from memory "The Lord's Prayer" and "Now I Lay Me Down to Sleep." The father wanted to make a good recording, so he made generous promises of candy when the job was done. At last her childish voice was being impressed perfectly on the record. The closing lines were recorded without a hitch:

If I should die before I wake
I pray the Lord my soul to take,
And this I ask for Jesus' sake.
Amen. Now give me my candy.

The final sentence came so quickly that the Father had no chance to stop the machine. Everything went on the record for posterity, including "This I ask for Jesus' sake. Amen. *Now* give me my candy."

What strange conclusions to prayers there are among children and among adults! You have been taught to say your prayers from memory. You repeat them hastily and often without meaning. You are anxious to get on to the next item of business—"Amen. *Now* give me my candy." What immediately follows your prayer is important.

There is seldom a refreshing pause between your prayers and your selfishness! Prayers become incidental to the big business at hand. Prayers become the bitterness in which you must indulge before you can have the sweets. Prayers become the demands a giant has made of you—so you obey and get it over with quickly and then do what you really want to do. Why pause after prayer? Why not reach out immediately for the thing you have been waiting for all the time anyway?

Because your prayers and what follows are going on the record for posterity. There's no getting away from that! There's no escaping it. The recording process cannot be stopped to allow time off for selfishness.

Do you remember grandmother Lois? Her life was

a record for posterity that was altogether wholesome. Paul pointed it out when he wrote to Timothy saying: "I am reminded of your sincere faith, a faith that dwelt first in your grandmother Lois and your mother Eunice and now, I am sure, dwells in you." Let's remember that your life and mine are being recorded for our children and our children's children.

Kneel Down–Look Up

> *O come, let us worship and bow down, let us kneel before the Lord, our Maker!*—Ps. 95:6.

Life had become very troubled for both of them. Together, this husband and wife looked out of the window of their little apartment in the big city. All they could see was a brick wall across the way. Then he said to her, "Let's kneel down and look up!" They knelt down by the window. Then they looked up and saw the clear sky beyond the brick wall.

Kneel down and look up. Don't just look up. To look up without kneeling down means that you will only see a ceiling or a brick wall. Bended knees make a difference. They bring the body a little lower in order that the mind may reach a little higher. The outlook changes when the knees are given their proper and rightful exercise. Kneel down and look up.

Kneel down and *look up*. Don't make the mistake of kneeling down and then looking down. When you are kneeling down and looking down you will see only the floor. You will see only more and more of man-made stuff. To kneel down and look up is to see God's sky. There are no floors and no walls and no fences in the sky. To look up is to look beyond all of the frustrations around you.

When you kneel down and look up there is nothing between you and God. Nobody that is anybody can put something between you and God. Should anyone ever dare to put something between you and God—then just kneel down and look up. When you do that you will want to pray, and prayer at a time like that will make a real difference.

Daniel, the Old Testament hero, did not live in a modern apartment house. Nevertheless "he went to his house where he had windows in his upper chamber open toward Jerusalem; and he got down upon his knees three times a day and prayed and gave thanks before his God" (Dan. 6:10). So Daniel found God beyond the man-made walls, floors, and ceilings.

Kneel down and look up!

Your Hands

> *What mighty works are wrought by his hands!*—Mark 6:2.

You fold your hands when you pray.
The right and the left of you,

Security from Above

The best and the worst in you,
Heaven and earth about you—
All *come* together when
You fold your hands and pray.

You fold your hands when you pray.
The clenched fist of anger,
The pointing finger of scorn,
The stubborn thumb of bitterness,
All *relax* together when
You fold your hands and pray.

You fold your hands when you pray.
Within the folded hands
Your fingers cross fingers,
Your crosses and the Cross,
All *aware* together when
You fold your hands and pray.

From your folded hands,
From your heart within,
From the Cross of Christ,
From the God above—
Love, forgiveness, peace,
All *bless* together when
You fold your hands and pray.

Silence

Be still, and know that I am God—Ps. 46:10.

There is nothing in all creation as much like God as silence—the sound of silence. Silence has a voice all its own, and this voice may be the voice of God. Have you ever been to church and there "let all the earth keep silence before him" (Hab. 2:20)? Silence is a good answer to all the earth's noises.

God works in silence. To be afraid of silence is to be afraid of God and what he is doing in life. Through silence God never betrays you—he just reminds you of how he works.

Love at its best comes, not with a shout, but in silence. You who have loved and who have been loved know this. Remember that God himself is love.

Mercy in all its tenderness comes not with a brassy band, but with meaningful forgiving silence. The mercies that are new each morning come as quietly as the daybreak.

Healing does not crackle and pop as it brings our wounded bodies and spirits back to health again. The great Physician comes and works confidently in silence.

Truth is powerful enough to make you free, and yet the life of truth depends not upon words or books or parades or sound of any kind. Truth lives by being that which it declares, being through the power of silence.

Faith comes by hearing, but hearing what? and hearing how? Faith comes by hearing the sound of silence, the still voice, the whispers of God.

Remember always and in all your ways that there is nothing, absolutely nothing in all creation as much like God as silence, silence because there may be nothing more to say.

Peace

> *Peace I leave with you; my peace I give to you*—John 14:27.

The peace you seek will come to you when you know the nature and the source of peace. Peace will attend your days and nights when you understand its possibilities amid unrest, strife, disorder.

Peace is very personal—it is communicated only from person to person. "Peace I leave with you; my peace I give to you." Peace cannot come through nature because nature is not at peace with itself. Animals may not possess the sensitive peace of which you may share. Peace will not come to you through mechanics, electronics, automation. Peace is the divine-human equation that looks at all of life in proper perspective. Peace is personal—intimately personal.

Peace is the steady assurance that overflows from one person to another person. It overflows impartially in all directions. Peace cannot keep itself to itself. Peace is never static. It is a living, moving relationship like a river attending the smooth and rough shorelines.

Peace is a gift you must take and use. "My peace I give to you" means nothing unless you believe the promise enough to take the gift and use it. You will use it (if you take it) in quietness and confidence. The gift of peace will adapt itself to your own personality, your own needs. But don't try to keep peace. The gift will return its value only if you share it as it was shared with you. Leave peace with others. Give peace to others. Be a peace-creator. "Blessed are the peace-makers" (Matt. 5:9).

Peace comes when you free yourself from all disagreement or quarrels with the Eternal. When your personal attitudes are in harmony with ultimate values, then will you be free from mental conflict and spiritual unrest. When you silently, quietly, serenely accept the Way, the Truth, the Life—then will you truly know peace.

Death

Death

> *Even though I walk through the*
> *valley of the shadow of death,*
> *I fear no evil;*
> *for thou art with me*—Ps. 23:4.

Sir Winston Leonard Spencer Churchill was given a state funeral with pomp and pageantry on January 30, 1965. It was reported that this event seen by thousands in London and by millions through television–this state event was in the planning stage twelve years before Churchill's death under the code name "Hope

Not." The precision of detail through the long procession reflected the years of planning that preceded it.

Do not hide from death. Let death come to you and for you. Resist not this stranger. There is pain in life but not in death. There is loneliness in life but not in death.

Death is neither fire nor ice. Death is neither all or nothing. Death is but a mending, a healing of life's ways. Death is your thanksgiving for the things you did not know before. Death is life's great adventure in awareness.

Those who have known death have no desire to return. To return is but to know death-bound life again. It is to know age, pain, frustration once more. To return is to return to fear—fear of death. You do not realize death until you live it. Then when you know it for what it is, it leaves you breathless. Death gives new life breathlessly.

Project yourself into death and you will find it is not death at all. You have projected yourself into the grave as if this were death. No grave can hold you. No earth can ever cover a living soul. No one can ever put you completely out of sight.

Death is the great offering you will make to God. This will be your all. Everything you *truly* possess you take into death. Your hands will be empty, but your life will be full.

Death is acceptable in God's sight, in the sight of our Lord, our Strength, and our Redeemer. Through death, God re-creates the earth and heaven. Through death, God takes the past and the present away so that there can be a future. Would you have it otherwise?

Smile into death. Let the grave echo with your laughter. Happily let death come. Others may mourn but you will not. Others will shed tears but you will not. Some may bid you "goodbye," but you will welcome yourself for what you are beyond death. Let death come to you and for you. It is impossible for you to imagine yourself out of existence forever. You can only think of yourself as being alive forevermore. Death is an experience in becoming more than you are. Let death come to you and for you, in God's own time and way.

"Excuse Me"

The time of my departure has come—II Tim. 4:6.

Death was just a moment away for this man. His friends were by his bedside. They knew. He knew. He just smiled, said, "Excuse me," and died. That was all he said, but it was rich in meaning for him and for his friends.

"Excuse me" was not said apologetically. It was said and understood as coming from a full Christlike life. It was another way of saying "The time of my departure has come." It is time to go, so "Excuse me."

This man was happily persuaded that his earthly visit had reached its limits. The conversation was beginning to drag. There wasn't much left to talk about. He was becoming uncomfortable, realizing that he had been around long enough. He knew his time had come and he was ready to go. Wonderful as this world had been, even with all its aches and pains, this was the moment he had been living for and toward. So, "Excuse me."

This man knew that he had been in the school of life. He had studied many subjects, some required, some elective. Some were mastered and others he failed. Having completed his earthly schooling, he was ready to graduate. He utterly believed in "higher education." Ready for postgraduate work, he simply said, "Excuse me," as he left his classmates. All the "undergraduates" understood!

It was just "Excuse me"—no more. This brief comment was sufficient. He knew they would have opportunity to talk with each other again. For to say, "Excuse me," is not to say we are through with each other. It is just that "The time of my departure has come" and so why linger around.

Have you ever thought about the moment when you will need to say, "Excuse me"? Why resist thinking about it? You can keep your hand on the doorknob waiting to go just so long. When it is time to go, it just is time to go! If you have "fought the good fight," if you "have kept the faith," then it will be a very gracious comfortable thing to smilingly look at your friends (and even your enemies) and say, "Excuse me."

Who knows when the time to say, "Excuse me," will come? No one. But it will come—that is a fact of life—yes, of *life*. Because it is at the moment of transition from life to more life when "the time of my departure has come" that it is time to say, "Excuse me."

Take-home Pay

> *Lay up for yourselves treasures in heaven*—Matt. 6:20.

What really counts is not what you earn, but your take-home pay. There are many people who have good incomes before all the deductions are made. But then after state and federal taxes, after union dues and social security, after hospitalization and other items are deducted, the take-home pay is considerably less than the salary that was earned. It is not the money you earn, but the pay you can take home that counts in today's world.

All of us have another home—a home in the skies. We call it our eternal heavenly home. What counts up there, too, is not what you have earned through the years but what you have left to take home with you. You can't take a bank account, nor a house, nor fine clothing with you. There are fourteen pockets in a man's three-piece suit, but all of them go empty into the grave.

Security from Above

The only thing you can take with you to the home beyond is what you truly are in terms of your faith, your hope, your love for God and man. That will constitute take-home pay. Take-home pay will consist of the ways in which you have been loyal to the person and the sayings of Jesus, to his teachings and his life.

It is a good thing to think seriously of the ultimate take-home pay as well as the weekly take-home pay. The federal and the state governments have nothing to do with the ultimate take-home pay. Neither the union nor all the insurance companies will have a voice in the matter. You alone will determine what the ultimate take-home pay will be. Will you be rich in character achievement? Will there be enough treasures within you in terms of good deeds and charity? Will your expressions of justice and fairness and honesty be something of which you will be proud or ashamed? Since heaven will be your final home, what are you doing now to make sure of adequate take-home pay, the kind of take-home pay that is an investment in security?

Using Immortality

> *I came, that they may have life, and have it abundantly*—John 10:10.

"If I cannot use worthily a single hour, what would be the meaning of immortality?" Ask yourself this question today and every day. "If I cannot use worthily a single hour, what would be the meaning of immortality?"

There are occasions when time hangs heavy on your hands. There are days when you just don't know what to do with yourself. The moments are dull and they do not hold promise of brightening up for you. Time drags. The minutes seem like hours. If life is like that for you now, how will you ever be able to make the adjustment to "endless moments" hereafter? If you cannot use this limited life span well, what can you do with the limitless life to come?

There are days that you misuse, abuse, refuse, or confuse! A misspent life is but an accumulation of misspent days. A day through which you sleep or daydream in apparent unconsciousness—that is a day refused. A day through which you have taken something simple and profound in the gospel and made it difficult to understand—that is a day you have confused for yourself and others. What would be the use of unending existence to a person who cannot use worthily a single hour?

Jesus died a young man. He lives as a young man throughout eternity. The immortality he presents is the immortality of a young man. His active ministry was one of the shortest pastorates on record. But so well did he use each hour while on earth in time that both heaven and earth declare he shall never die. Jesus got his training for the future by using the present worthily. He invested his life in time that it might bear fruit in eternity.

Jesus said, "I came, that they may have life, and have it abundantly." You have life—you use life—but how well do you use it? You will have more life as you use it well, until beyond this horizon you have life in all its abundance. You will learn how to use immortality when you learn how to use worthily each hour for the God you worship and love.

Dust

You are dust, and to dust you shall return—Gen. 3:19.

You are dust
And to dust you shall return.
The Lord God formed man
Of dust from the ground:
The lowliest stuff,
The most unpromising substance
Beneath his feet—
Molded to receive his breath
Man—a living soul!

O Man, dust you are,
Not gold but dust,
Not costly but cheap,
Not scarce but plentiful:
Without price in any market,
There are no quotations on dust.
Damager, disturber, disintegrator;
Target of heaven and hell.
Dust you are.

Black dust,
Black as the oozing, spongy muck
Of the soft, decaying swamp.
Swarthy, somber, forbidding.
Absorbing all light rays.
Black as the *Negro.*
Dust you are.

Red dust,
Red as the firm burnt clay.
Sun-tinted red, dull pale red.
Angry, radical, revolutionary.
At the lower end of the spectrum.
Red as the coppery skinned *Red Man,*
Dust you are.

Brown dust,
Brown as the earth
Of the plot in your own back yard.
Giving much from very little,
Dirty, earthy, faded brown.
Brown as the sun-baked *man of Arabia,*
Dust you are.

Yellow dust,
Yellow as the barren prairies
The ranchers know.
Yielding little, giving begrudgingly—
Pale, brittle, sick, jaundiced.
Yellow as the *Mongolian,*
Dust you are.

White dust,
White as the sands on the shores.
Deceptively clean and smooth
Yet bland, bleached, betraying sand.
Reflecting all light rays.
Yet loose and gritty as the *White Man,*
Dust you are.

Gray dust,
Old, unbleached, dreary.
Mixed, hoary, uncomplementary.
Covering a deserted playground,
Imperfectly absorbing all light rays.
Part of all dust, blend of all races,
Still—dust you are.

O Man,
Burn this in your calloused flesh:
You are dust
And to dust all men return.
Dust—yes, dust without which:
No brilliant sunrise, no glowing sunset,
No falling rain, no rainbow arch.

To dust all men return.
Rising as the dust rises,
Falling as the dust falls.
Great and small; in everything, over everything.
Black, red, brown, yellow, white, gray dust.
But still dust, dusty dust,
Yet hopeful dust.

To dust all men return,
Working together in death
If not in life.
Urged by war and hate
Rather than by peace and goodwill;
Compelled by death and time,
Unimpelled by life and immortality

You are dust,
And to dust you shall return.
The Lord God formed man
Of dust from the ground.
The lowliest stuff,
The most unpromising substance
Beneath his feet
Received the Master Potter's touch,
And by his breath—a living soul!

Dust you are,
Living in hope of him,
Him whose dusty body was broken,
Broken to be born a new body out of the dust;
Out of the dust the Baby.
Out of the dust the Crucifixion.
Out of the dust the Resurrection!

Eternity

He has put eternity into man's mind—Eccl. 3:11.

You came out of eternity, you live within eternity, and into eternity you go. You are at one with eternity and possess a distinctive feeling for the everlasting. You have it! Ultimately, you are independent of time.

You would know and be known more and more. The will to know the inmost and the uttermost is at one with eternity. You possess that will—do not let it go. You have known only fragments of your being. There is your whole eternal being yet to know and be known. There are others too, to know to the uttermost.

You would love and be loved more and more. The touch of divine love you have known has been made sensitive by the human love you have missed. You have found only the hem of Love's garment. Love is for you forever.

You would live and live abundantly. The dehydrated life you have known is not to be compared with the life that is to be. The "golden" memorable moments in time are but foretastes of the "golden" streets of the eternal city.

You would be your self, your best self, your fullest self forever. You have a name, an identity. You are a distinctive person unlike anyone else in the past, the present, or future. You have sought to be, tried to be your self through time. The dates of time: birthdays, deadlines, demanded payments, dreaded appointments—these calendared frustrations have prevented you from being your self. But you are at one with eternity, and in eternity there are no dates—you will be your fullest self, your best self forever. You will know the Everlasting Mercy.

You are a native of the everlasting. The feeling you have for eternity comes from insight, not from sight. It comes from intuition, not from reason. It comes from your heart, not from your head. Adjust your life to the native within you.

You are an heir of the eternal God and a fellow heir with Christ. "I am sure that neither death, nor life, nor angels, nor principalities, nor things present, nor things to come, nor powers, nor height, nor depth, nor anything else in all creation, will be able to separate us from the love of God in Christ Jesus our Lord" (Rom. 8:38-39).

You are at one with eternity—with the more that you are, with the security coming from above.

Not yet—"It does not yet appear what we shall be" (I John 3:2). Not yet.